The 7-Figure Blueprint

A Step-by-Step Field Manual for Building a Real Estate Wholesaling Business

By
Doran Newton

Copyright © 2024 Doran Newton. All rights reserved.

No part of this publication may be reproduced, distributed, or transmitted in any form or by any means, including photocopying, recording, or other electronic or mechanical methods, without the prior written permission of the publisher, except in the case of brief quotations embodied in critical reviews and certain other noncommercial uses permitted by copyright law.

Disclaimer

The information provided in this book is for general informational purposes only. While the author and publisher have made every effort to ensure the accuracy and completeness of the information conveyed in this publication, they do not assume and hereby disclaim any liability to any party for any loss, damage, or disruption caused by errors or omissions, whether such errors or omissions result from negligence, accident, or any other cause.

This book is intended to provide a general overview of the author's views concerning the subject matter and is not intended as professional advice or services. Readers are advised to consult a professional or specialist before making any business decision.

This publication is not intended for use as a source of legal, business, accounting, or financial advice. All readers are advised to seek services of competent professionals in legal, business, accounting, and finance fields.

Author: Doran Newton

Table Of Contents

Preface
- Introduction to the Author
- How to Use This Book

Part I: Foundations of Real Estate Wholesaling
- Chapter 1: Introduction to Real Estate Wholesaling
- Chapter 2: Legal and Regulatory Essentials

Part II: Launching Your Business
- Chapter 3: Setting Up Your Business Structure
- Chapter 4: Tools and Technology for Effective Operations

Part III: Financial Management
- Chapter 5: Exploring Financing Options
- Chapter 6: Cash Flow and Financial Operations

Part IV: Development and Networking
- Chapter 7: Building a Robust Professional Network
- Chapter 8: Working with Real Estate Agents and Other Professionals

Part V: The Art of the Deal
- Chapter 9: Finding and Acquiring Properties
- Chapter 10: Mastering Property Valuation

Conclusion
- Recap and Encouraging Future Growth

About the Author

Introduction

Welcome to "The Step-By-Step Field Manual For Building A 7-Figure Real Estate Wholesaling Business," your comprehensive guide to entering and succeeding in the dynamic world of real estate wholesaling. Whether you are a seasoned entrepreneur looking to expand into new ventures or a newcomer eager to carve out a profitable niche, this book is designed to equip you with the knowledge, strategies, and insights needed to launch and grow a successful real estate wholesaling business.

Real estate wholesaling stands as one of the most straightforward, yet profoundly effective entry points into the world of real estate investment. It involves contracting a home with a seller and then finding an interested party to buy it. The wholesaler sells the contract to a buyer, making a profit on the difference between the contracted price with the seller and the amount the buyer pays. This process requires little to no money down, making it an attractive strategy for those without significant capital but with a keen sense of the market.

However, as accessible as wholesaling can be, its simplicity is deceptive. The market's complexity, legal intricacies, financial considerations, and the need for a solid operational strategy can turn what seems like a straightforward venture into a labyrinth of decisions and risks. This book is here to guide you through that labyrinth.

In this field manual, we will cover every aspect of building a successful wholesaling business. From setting up your business legally and effectively, understanding the intricacies of real estate law, to mastering the art of deal-finding and negotiation, every part has been structured to provide step-by-step guidance. Additionally, we delve into the essential practices for financing your operations, managing cash flow, and scaling your business sustainably.

This book is divided into several parts, each focusing on a specific aspect of the wholesaling business:
- Part I introduces you to the basics of real estate wholesaling, laying the groundwork for what wholesaling is and why it is a viable business strategy.
- Part II guides you through the initial steps of setting up and structuring your business.
- Part III focuses on the financial aspects of wholesaling, including how to finance deals and manage your cash flow.
- Part IV enhances your understanding of networking and developing beneficial relationships within the real estate industry.
- Part V and Part VI cover the operational aspects of sourcing deals, negotiating, closing, and eventually scaling your operations.
- - Part VII tackles the critical elements of risk management to ensure your business thrives in various market conditions.

By the end of this book, you will have gained not only foundational knowledge but also practical tools and strategies to build a robust, profitable real estate wholesaling business. Let's embark on this journey together, turning opportunities into successful deals and transforming your entrepreneurial vision into a lucrative reality.

How To Use This Book

Welcome to "The Step-By-Step Field Manual For Building A 7-Figure Real Estate Wholesaling Business." Whether you're diving into real estate wholesaling for the first time or looking to enhance your existing business, this book is structured to guide you through every crucial step, ensuring you understand both the strategic and operational aspects of real estate wholesaling. Below, I'll outline how to maximize the benefit of this book, making your reading experience both enlightening and practical.

The book is divided into several parts, each dedicated to a different facet of building a successful real estate wholesaling business. Each part contains chapters that delve deeper into specific topics. Start by skimming through the Table of Contents to get a sense of the book's structure and the breadth of topics covered. This will help you identify the sections most relevant to your current needs and interests.

While this book is designed to be read sequentially—from laying the foundational knowledge and skills needed in early chapters to more advanced concepts in later ones—it's also crafted to allow you to jump directly to topics of immediate relevance. For example, if you are already familiar with the basics of real estate wholesaling, you might choose to focus on parts about scaling a business or managing financial operations. Use the index to find specific topics quickly.

Throughout the book, you'll find various tools and templates designed to facilitate your learning and application of the concepts discussed. These include checklists, worksheets, and sample documents that can be directly implemented into your business practices. Make sure to use these resources to their fullest—either by printing them out from the digital version of the book or photocopying them if you're using a physical copy.

To enhance your understanding, this book includes numerous case studies and real-world examples of successful real estate deals. Analyze these examples to see theoretical concepts put into practice. This real-world application can help bridge the gap between theory and practice, providing a clearer picture of how decisions are made and executed in the field.

As you read through each chapter, take the time to reflect on how the information applies to your personal situation and jot down any ideas or questions that arise. Keeping a notebook or a digital document for notes and thoughts related to each chapter can be incredibly helpful. This not only aids in retaining information but also in applying the book's insights to your own business planning and operations.

After your initial read-through, use this book as a reference guide. The world of real estate is dynamic, and as you grow in your career, you will find that different sections of the book become relevant at different times. Regularly revisiting chapters as you come across new challenges or opportunities can provide fresh insights and guidance.

Consider joining online forums, local meetups, or other communities of real estate professionals discussed in this book. Engaging with others in the field can provide support, deepen your understanding, and offer networking opportunities. Share your learnings and experiences based on the book's teachings, and learn from others who are on the same journey.

By following these guidelines, you can maximize your use of "The Step-By-Step Field Manual For Building A 7-Figure Real Estate Wholesaling Business" to not only learn about real estate wholesaling but also to effectively implement these strategies in real-life scenarios. Here's to building a successful and sustainable business!

Part I: Foundations of Real Estate Wholesaling

Welcome to the exciting world of real estate wholesaling! In this introduction, we will delve into the foundations of this lucrative investment strategy that has gained popularity among savvy investors and entrepreneurs. Real estate wholesaling serves as a gateway to the dynamic and ever-evolving property market where potential profits await those who understand its intricacies.

Real estate wholesaling involves connecting motivated sellers with eager buyers without the need for direct ownership or extensive financial resources. Instead, wholesalers act as intermediaries, skillfully navigating the market to find great deals and secure profitable transactions. By capitalizing on market inefficiencies, wholesalers can create win-win scenarios for all parties involved.

The foundation of real estate wholesaling is built upon a few key principles. Firstly, thorough market research and analysis play a vital role in identifying neighborhoods with potential, understanding local market trends, and gauging demand for certain types of properties. This knowledge allows wholesalers to spot opportunities and target their efforts effectively.

Additionally, cultivating a network of contacts in the industry becomes crucial for wholesalers. Building relationships with motivated sellers, investors, real estate agents, and other professionals involved in the property market can provide a steady flow of leads and valuable insights. The ability to negotiate and communicate effectively is paramount, as wholesalers must strike deals that benefit both sellers and buyers.

Another essential foundation of real estate wholesaling is the ability to accurately estimate property values. Wholesalers must have a keen eye for evaluating the condition, location, and potential market value of properties. By accurately assessing a property's worth, wholesalers can confidently negotiate deals that align with their profit goals.

Furthermore, a thorough understanding of legal requirements and contracts is vital to navigate the intricacies of real estate transactions. Wholesalers must ensure compliance with local regulations and employ proper documentation to protect all parties involved in the transaction.

In this captivating journey into the foundations of real estate wholesaling, we will explore various strategies and techniques that empower wholesalers to succeed in this competitive market. From finding off-market properties and negotiating favorable deals to building a trusted network and mastering the art of marketing, real estate wholesaling presents endless possibilities for entrepreneurs and investors looking to generate profits.

So, embrace the world of real estate wholesaling and discover how this innovative approach unlocks a realm of opportunities in the dynamic property market. This guide aims to equip you with the knowledge and tools needed to thrive in the exciting and rewarding world of real estate wholesaling.

Chapter 1: Introduction to Real Estate Wholesaling

Real estate wholesaling is an investment strategy that has gained significant popularity in the real estate industry. It involves acting as a middleman between motivated sellers and buyers, facilitating the transfer of properties without actually taking ownership. Wholesalers focus on finding great deals, negotiating favorable terms, and then assigning the contract to an interested buyer for a fee. This strategy allows investors to generate profits without the need for extensive financial resources or long-term ownership commitments.

Explanation of Real Estate Wholesaling:
In real estate wholesaling, the main objective is to identify distressed or undervalued properties, negotiate with the owners, and secure them under a purchase contract at a lower price. The wholesaler then markets the property to potential buyers, often other investors, at a higher price, incorporating their own profit margin. Once an interested buyer is found, the wholesaler assigns the contract to the buyer, who takes over the obligations and benefits of the original purchase agreement.

Unlike traditional real estate investing strategies, such as rental properties or fix-and-flip projects, wholesaling does not involve renovations, property management, or long-term ownership. Instead, it focuses on the efficient transfer of properties, capitalizing on the discrepancies between motivated sellers seeking quick sales and buyers seeking profitable deals.

Brief Comparison with Other Real Estate Investment Strategies:
Real estate wholesaling stands out among other investment strategies in several ways. Let's briefly compare it to some common real estate investment approaches:

1. Rental Properties: Many investors choose to buy properties as rental investments, aiming for long-term cash flow and potential appreciation. However, rental properties require substantial financial investment, property management responsibilities, and involvement in tenant-related issues. In contrast, wholesaling allows investors to generate profits without the burdens of ownership and long-term management.

2. Fix-and-Flip: Fix-and-flip investments involve purchasing distressed properties, renovating them, and selling them for a profit. While this approach can be lucrative, it requires significant capital, time, and expertise in construction and project management. Real estate wholesaling, on the other hand, allows investors to capitalize on opportunities without the need for renovations or extensive property improvements.

3. Buy-and-Hold: Buy-and-hold investors focus on acquiring properties with the intention of holding them for an extended period, benefiting from rental income and potential appreciation over time. This strategy requires long-term commitment, active property management, and a solid understanding of market trends. Real estate wholesaling provides a more streamlined and faster process for investors seeking quicker profits and less involvement.

4. Flipping Contracts: Flipping contracts, often referred to as contract assignment, is similar to wholesaling. Both involve assigning purchase contracts to other buyers. However, real estate wholesaling encompasses a broader range of activities, including identifying and negotiating deals, marketing properties, and building a network of contacts. Wholesaling provides investors with more opportunities to generate consistent income from multiple transactions.

In summary, real estate wholesaling offers a unique investment strategy that allows investors to generate profits through the efficient transfer of properties without the long-term commitments and responsibilities of traditional investment approaches. It provides an avenue for investors to enter the real estate market with less capital and risk, offering flexibility and the potential for quick returns. As the chapter progresses, we will delve deeper into the intricate aspects of real estate wholesaling, equipping you with the knowledge and skills necessary for success in this exciting investment strategy.

How Wholesaling Works:
Real estate wholesaling involves a step-by-step process that enables investors to profit from the transfer of properties without actually taking ownership. Let's explore the key components of how wholesaling works, from finding properties to closing the deal.

Step-by-Step Process:

1. Finding Properties: The first step in wholesaling is to identify potential properties for investment. This involves thorough market research, networking with industry professionals, scouring online listings, attending auctions, and exploring distressed property databases. The goal is to locate properties that are undervalued, in need of quick sales, or have motivated sellers.

2. Securing Contracts: Once a potential property is identified, the wholesaler must negotiate and secure a purchase contract with the owner. This often involves conducting thorough due diligence, assessing the property's condition, evaluating market value, and negotiating mutually beneficial terms with the seller. The purchase contract should include contingency clauses, allowing the wholesaler to have an escape route if needed.

3. Finding Buyers: With a property under contract, the next step is to find interested buyers who are willing to purchase the property from the wholesaler. This entails building a network of investors, attending real estate investment meetings, leveraging online marketing platforms, and showcasing the potential of the property. Effective marketing strategies, such as creating enticing property profiles, utilizing social media, and reaching out to investment groups, can attract potential buyers.

4. Presenting the Deal: Once potential buyers express interested in the property, the wholesaler must present the deal in a compelling and transparent manner. This includes providing comprehensive property details, such as photos, property information, repair estimates (if needed), and potential profit projections. The wholesaler should also clearly outline the terms of the purchase contract and the assignment fee, which is the wholesaler's profit.

5. Assigning the Contract: When a buyer agrees to the terms and expresses intent to proceed, the wholesaler assigns the purchase contract to the buyer. This transfer of rights involves an assignment

agreement, which legally assigns the obligations and benefits of the purchase contract to the buyer. The wholesaler receives an agreed-upon assignment fee, typically paid by the buyer at closing.

6. Closing the Deal: The final step in the wholesaling process is the closing of the deal. The buyer proceeds with the purchase, and the closing takes place at a designated title company or attorney's office. The wholesaler's assignment fee is typically paid at this stage. The title company ensures that all legal and financial aspects of the transaction are handled appropriately, transferring ownership from the seller to the buyer.

Role of the Wholesaler in the Real Estate Market:
Wholesalers play a significant role in the real estate market, acting as intermediaries between motivated sellers and buyers seeking investment opportunities. Their key responsibilities include:

1. Identifying Opportunities: Wholesalers diligently search for undervalued or distressed properties and locate motivated sellers who need quick sales due to various reasons, such as financial distress, inheritance, or relocation.

2. Creating Win-Win Solutions: By negotiating favorable terms with sellers and securing properties at a lower price, wholesalers create win-win situations. Sellers can achieve a quick sale, while buyers can access discounted properties with potential for profit.

3. Providing Value to Buyers: Wholesalers offer investors access to a curated list of discounted properties that have already undergone initial evaluation. This saves buyers time and effort in searching for suitable investment opportunities.

4. Facilitating Efficient Transactions: Wholesalers streamline the transaction process by handling paperwork, coordinating with title

companies, and ensuring a smooth transition of ownership, allowing buyers to focus on their investment strategies.

5. Building Networks: Successful wholesalers build extensive networks of motivated sellers, buyers, real estate agents, lenders, and other industry professionals. These networks facilitate the flow of deals and enable wholesalers to connect buyers with suitable properties.

In summary, wholesalers play a vital role in the real estate market by identifying lucrative investment opportunities, connecting motivated sellers with interested buyers, and facilitating the transfer of properties. By streamlining the transaction process and providing value to both sellers and buyers, wholesalers contribute to the efficiency and dynamism of the real estate investment landscape.

Benefits of Real Estate Wholesaling

Real estate wholesaling offers several unique benefits that set it apart from traditional real estate investments. Let's explore these advantages, including low entry barriers and the potential for quick returns.

Low Entry Barriers:
One of the most attractive aspects of real estate wholesaling is the low entry barriers it presents, both financially and educationally. Unlike other investment strategies that often require significant capital and specialized knowledge, wholesaling allows individuals with limited financial resources and experience to participate in the real estate market. As a wholesaler, you can leverage deals without the need for substantial upfront investment and instead focus on finding and negotiating profitable opportunities. This accessibility makes real estate wholesaling an appealing option for aspiring investors looking to enter the market.

Potential for Quick Returns:

Real estate wholesaling also offers the potential for quick returns compared to traditional real estate investments. When you engage in wholesaling, you are not tied to long-term ownership or rental income. Instead, you aim to find motivated sellers and connect them with interested buyers who are willing to pay a premium for the property. By capitalizing on the price discrepancies and facilitating speedy transactions, you can generate profits within a short period. This ability to realize returns quickly makes wholesaling an attractive strategy for investors seeking liquidity and faster financial gains.

Moreover, as a real estate wholesaler, you have the flexibility to engage in multiple transactions simultaneously. With a streamlined process that focuses on finding, negotiating, and assigning contracts, you can often work on several deals concurrently. This allows you to maximize your earning potential and increase your chances of achieving consistent profits. By leveraging your expanding network of buyers and sellers, you can explore various opportunities, diversify your portfolio, and amplify your returns.

Additionally, real estate wholesaling provides a valuable learning experience. As you navigate the market, you gain practical knowledge about property evaluation, negotiation skills, market analysis, and networking. This knowledge can be transferrable to other real estate investment strategies if you decide to venture into long-term ownership, fix-and-flip projects, or buy-and-hold investments in the future.

In summary, real estate wholesaling offers several noteworthy benefits that make it an appealing investment strategy. The low entry barriers, both financially and educationally, enable individuals with limited resources to participate in the market. The potential for quick returns, compared to traditional real estate investments, allows wholesalers to capitalize on price discrepancies and generate profits within a shorter timeframe. Embracing wholesaling not only provides financial opportunities but also equips investors with valuable industry knowledge and skills that can be applied to other real estate endeavors.

Real estate wholesaling, while offering enticing benefits, also comes with its fair share of challenges. In this section, we will explore two key challenges faced by wholesalers: market dependence and variability, as well as legal and ethical considerations.

Market Dependence and Variability:
Wholesalers are inherently dependent on the real estate market's dynamics, making it necessary to adapt to market changes. The demand for properties, buyer preferences, and market trends can fluctuate, affecting wholesaling opportunities. Economic factors, such as interest rates, unemployment rates, and local market conditions, can impact the supply and demand for properties, influencing the feasibility of wholesaling deals. Wholesalers must stay attuned to market changes, monitor industry news, and continually assess the viability of their investments.

Moreover, the variability within the real estate market introduces its own set of challenges. Wholesaling opportunities can vary significantly depending on the location, type of property, and market conditions. Wholesalers must be prepared to encounter fluctuations in property values, sales cycles, and buyer demand. These variations may require wholesalers to adjust their strategies, refine their target markets, and actively seek out opportunities in areas with higher demand and potential profitability. Adapting to market fluctuations and tailoring strategies accordingly is essential to thrive as a wholesaler.

Legal and Ethical Considerations:
Wholesalers must navigate the legal and ethical considerations associated with their business practices. While wholesaling is a legitimate investment strategy, it is crucial to operate within the confines of legal regulations and maintain ethical standards. Some key considerations include:

1. Assignment and Agreement Compliance: Wholesalers must ensure that their activities comply with local laws and regulations governing real estate transactions. This includes adhering to contract

assignment rules, disclosing their role as wholesalers, and ensuring all necessary documentation is completed accurately and transparently.

2. Disclosure and Transparency: Wholesalers should maintain clear and open communication with both sellers and buyers, disclosing their intentions and the potential assignment of the contract. Transparency is crucial to avoid misunderstandings and build trust among parties involved in the transaction.

3. Fair and Honest Dealings: Wholesalers should conduct their business with fairness and honesty, avoiding misleading or deceptive practices. This entails accurately representing the property, disclosing any known issues, and providing reliable information to buyers and sellers.

4. Compliance with Marketing Regulations: Wholesalers' marketing efforts should adhere to advertising and fair housing regulations. It is essential to avoid making false claims, engage in discriminatory practices, or violate any legal requirements related to marketing real estate properties.

5. Engaging Licensed Professionals: Wholesalers may need to collaborate with licensed real estate agents, attorneys, or title companies to ensure the legality and smooth execution of transactions. Consulting professionals can help navigate complex legal procedures and ensure compliance with regulations.

By maintaining a strong commitment to legal and ethical considerations, wholesalers can safeguard their reputation, build long-term relationships within the industry, and mitigate potential risks or legal issues.

In summary, wholesalers encounter challenges related to market dependence and variability, as well as legal and ethical considerations. Adapting to changing market conditions, staying informed about industry trends, and being flexible in approach are crucial for success in wholesaling. Furthermore, adhering to legal regulations, maintaining transparency, and conducting business ethically are essential practices to uphold the integrity of the wholesaling profession. By addressing these challenges proactively, wholesalers can position themselves for sustainable growth and profitability in the real estate market.

To excel in the field of real estate wholesaling, acquiring specific skills and utilizing appropriate tools is crucial. This section will highlight the essential skills and tools that contribute to success in wholesaling.

Essential Skills:

1. Networking: Building a strong network is vital for wholesalers. Creating connections with real estate agents, investors, property owners, and other industry professionals can provide a continuous source of potential deals and buyers. Networking events, real estate associations, and online communities are excellent platforms to expand your network and establish valuable relationships.

2. Negotiation: Proficiency in negotiation is a skill that wholesalers must master. Effective negotiation allows wholesalers to secure favorable deals, obtain the best possible prices, and convince both buyers and sellers of the mutual benefits of a transaction. Developing strong communication, active listening, and problem-solving abilities are key components of successful negotiation.

3. Market Analysis: A thorough understanding of the real estate market is essential for wholesalers to identify profitable opportunities. Conducting market analysis involves researching local trends, analyzing property values, vacancy rates, rental yields, and assessing the demand and supply dynamics. This knowledge helps wholesalers identify target markets, assess property values, and determine potential profitability.

Tools:

1. CRM Software: Customer Relationship Management (CRM) software is an invaluable tool for wholesalers to manage their contacts, leads, and transactions effectively. A CRM system helps organize buyer and seller information, schedule follow-ups, track communication history, and streamline the workflow. It enables wholesalers to stay organized, enhance customer relationships, and improve overall productivity.

2. Property Analysis Tools: Wholesalers rely on property analysis tools to evaluate the financial viability of potential deals. These tools assist in estimating property values, assessing repair costs, and calculating potential profits. Property analysis software and spreadsheets can automate complex calculations, provide detailed reports, and enable wholesalers to make informed decisions based on accurate data.

3. Marketing Strategies: Wholesalers need effective marketing strategies to attract both motivated sellers and interested buyers. Utilizing various marketing techniques, such as online advertising, social media promotions, direct mail campaigns, and targeted marketing to specific buyer demographics, is crucial to connect with the right audience. Implementing analytics tools to track the performance of marketing campaigns can help wholesalers refine their strategies and optimize their marketing efforts.

By honing essential skills such as networking, negotiation, and market analysis, wholesalers can position themselves as industry experts and maximize their success. Additionally, leveraging tools like CRM software, property analysis tools, and marketing strategies enhances efficiency, organization, and effectiveness in wholesaling operations.

In summary, possessing key skills such as networking, negotiation, and market analysis is essential for success in real estate wholesaling. These skills enable wholesalers to build valuable connections, negotiate profitable deals, and make informed investment decisions. Furthermore, utilizing tools like CRM software, property analysis tools, and effective marketing strategies enhances productivity, accuracy, and marketing reach. Mastery of both skills and tools equips wholesalers to navigate the dynamic real estate market and thrive in their wholesaling endeavors.

Operating within a clear legal framework and ensuring compliance is critical for wholesalers in the real estate industry. This section will explore the basic legal requirements for wholesaling and emphasize the importance of understanding local real estate laws.

Basic Legal Requirements for Wholesaling:

1. Licensing: In some jurisdictions, wholesalers may be required to hold a real estate license to conduct wholesaling activities. It is essential to research and understand the licensing requirements in the specific area of operation. Compliance with licensing regulations ensures legality and protects wholesalers from potential legal consequences.

2. Contractual Agreements: Wholesaling involves entering into contractual agreements with property sellers and buyers. These agreements typically include an assignment contract, allowing the wholesaler to transfer their contractual rights to a buyer. Wholesalers must ensure that these agreements comply with local laws and regulations, including contract validity, assignment clauses, and proper disclosure of their role in the transaction.

3. Disclosure Requirements: Wholesalers have a responsibility to disclose any material facts or information regarding the property to both sellers and buyers. This includes disclosing known defects, liens, or other important details that may affect the property's value or marketability. Failure to disclose such information can lead to legal liabilities and potential financial consequences.

4. Advertising and Marketing Regulations: Wholesalers must adhere to advertising and marketing regulations specific to the real estate industry. These regulations aim to prevent false advertising, misleading representations, or discriminatory practices. Wholesalers should ensure that their marketing materials, including property listings, advertising campaigns, and promotional content, comply with local laws and ethical standards.

Importance of Understanding Local Real Estate Laws:

Comprehending and adhering to local real estate laws is crucial for wholesalers. The legal landscape governing real estate transactions can vary significantly from one jurisdiction to another. Some important reasons why wholesalers must understand local laws include:

1. Legal Compliance: Understanding local real estate laws ensures that wholesalers operate within the legal boundaries of their jurisdiction. Compliance with licensing requirements, contract laws, disclosure obligations, and advertising regulations protects wholesalers from legal penalties, disputes, or voided contracts.

2. Risk Mitigation: Knowledge of local laws helps wholesalers identify and mitigate potential legal risks associated with their business activities. By understanding the legal requirements and potential pitfalls, wholesalers can take appropriate precautions, seek legal advice when necessary, and minimize the likelihood of legal complications.

3. Reputation and Trust: Operating in accordance with local real estate laws enhances a wholesaler's reputation and fosters trust among sellers, buyers, and other industry professionals. Demonstrating ethical conduct and compliance with legal requirements establishes wholesalers as trustworthy and reliable business partners within the real estate community.

4. Market Knowledge: Local real estate laws often reflect the unique characteristics of a specific market. By understanding these laws, wholesalers gain insights into market dynamics, contractual norms, and legal procedures. This knowledge helps wholesalers make informed decisions, negotiate effectively, and adapt to the local market environment.

In summary, wholesalers must adhere to basic legal requirements, including licensing, contractual obligations, disclosure obligations, and compliance with advertising regulations. Understanding local real estate laws is crucial for legal compliance, risk mitigation, reputation building, and gaining market knowledge. By operating within a clear legal framework and demonstrating a commitment to compliance, wholesalers can establish themselves as reputable professionals in the real estate industry.

Chapter 6: Case Studies and Examples

Real estate wholesaling can be a highly lucrative venture when approached strategically and executed effectively. This section will delve into real-life examples of successful real estate wholesaling deals and highlight the valuable lessons learned from these case studies.

Case Study 1: The Distressed Property Flip

In this case study, a wholesaler identified a distressed property in a rapidly appreciating neighborhood. The property was in need of significant repairs, and the seller was motivated to sell quickly. The wholesaler negotiated a favorable purchase price and secured the property under contract.

Timing and Market Awareness
The success of this deal was attributed to the wholesaler's keen market awareness and timing. By identifying a distressed property in an up-and-coming area, the wholesaler capitalized on the potential for future appreciation. This case study emphasizes the importance of staying

informed about market trends, identifying undervalued properties, and seizing opportunities when they arise.

Case Study 2: The Off-Market Deal

In this example, a wholesaler leveraged their extensive network and relationships to secure an off-market property deal. Through networking events, the wholesaler connected with a motivated seller who was willing to sell his property below market value due to personal circumstances. The wholesaler quickly negotiated a deal and assigned the contract to an interested buyer for a profit.

Networking and Relationship Building
This case study highlights the power of networking and cultivating relationships within the real estate industry. Building a strong network can provide access to off-market deals, exclusive opportunities, and motivated sellers. Wholesalers should prioritize growing their connections and establishing a reputation as a reliable and professional partner.

Case Study 3: The Multiple Exit Strategies

In this scenario, a wholesaler encountered a property that had both exceptional wholesale and fix-and-flip potential. Recognizing the versatility of the property, the wholesaler pursued multiple exit strategies. They initially marketed the property to potential cash investors interested in wholesaling. Simultaneously, they also explored the possibility of renovating the property for a higher profit. Ultimately, the wholesaler was able to secure a wholesale deal, but also had a backup plan in case it fell through.

Flexibility and Creativity
This case study emphasizes the importance of flexibility and creativity in real estate wholesaling. Wholesalers should be open to exploring various exit strategies based on the unique characteristics of the property and the

market conditions. Being adaptable and considering alternative options can maximize the potential for profit and mitigate risks.

In summary, real-life case studies provide valuable insights into successful real estate wholesaling deals. Learning from these examples, we understand the importance of market awareness, timing, networking, relationship building, flexibility, and creativity. By incorporating these lessons into their wholesaling strategies, wholesalers can increase their chances of identifying profitable deals, securing favorable contracts, and maximizing their profits in the dynamic real estate market.

Throughout this guide, we have delved into the intricacies of real estate wholesaling, covering a wide range of essential topics, strategies, and considerations. As we reach the conclusion of this journey, let us take a moment to recap the key essentials and pave the way for the next chapter focused on setting up a legal and effective business structure.

First and foremost, we explored the crucial aspect of finding motivated sellers. Understanding different avenues, such as direct marketing, networking, and online platforms, enables wholesalers to locate properties with potential profit opportunities. By honing the skill of identifying motivated sellers, wholesalers gain a competitive edge in the market.

Next, we dived into the art of identifying profitable deals. Analyzing market trends, evaluating property values, assessing repair costs, and considering factors like location and demand contribute to making informed decisions on which properties to pursue. The ability to spot lucrative opportunities is a vital skill that wholesalers should cultivate.

Effective negotiation skills are another indispensable attribute for successful wholesalers. The ability to communicate persuasively, build rapport, and leverage information can result in favorable purchase prices and terms. Mastering the art of negotiation strengthens wholesalers' position and increases their chances of securing profitable contracts.

Managing the transaction process is a critical aspect of wholesaling. Coordinating with sellers, buyers, title companies, and other stakeholders requires exceptional organizational skills and attention to detail. From contract to closing, wholesalers need to navigate the process efficiently and professionally.

Understanding the legal framework and compliance requirements is crucial for wholesalers to operate within the bounds of the law. Familiarizing oneself with local regulations, disclosure obligations, and ethical practices ensures a smooth and legally sound business operation.

Incorporating market awareness, timing, networking, relationship building, flexibility, and creativity are also valuable attributes for wholesalers. Staying informed about market trends and timing property acquisitions strategically can maximize returns. Building a network of industry professionals and establishing strong relationships may lead to off-market deals and collaborations. Being adaptable and creative allows wholesalers to explore different exit strategies and adapt to changing market conditions.

As we look ahead to the next chapter, we anticipate exploring the realm of setting up a legal and effective business structure. This chapter will delve into the various business entity types, registration requirements, tax implications, and other considerations necessary to establish a solid foundation for a successful wholesaling business.

By establishing a strong legal and business structure, wholesalers can operate with confidence, ensuring compliance with regulations and positioning themselves as reliable and professional players in the real estate industry.

We invite you to stay tuned for the upcoming chapter, where we will delve deeper into the intricacies of setting up a legal and effective business structure in the realm of real estate wholesaling.

Chapter 2: Legal and Regulatory Essentials

Real estate wholesaling can be a highly profitable business, but it's important to navigate the legal and regulatory landscape to avoid legal troubles. Compliance with relevant laws is crucial for wholesalers to maintain their reputation and ensure long-term success. This chapter will provide an overview of real estate law, including the laws that impact wholesaling, and emphasize the importance of compliance in this business.

Overview of Relevant Laws Affecting Real Estate Wholesaling:

Real estate wholesaling is subject to several laws and regulations that wholesalers must be familiar with. Some of the key laws include:

1. RESPA (Real Estate Settlement Procedures Act): This legislation governs the settlement process in real estate transactions. It requires sellers and buyers to receive specific disclosures at certain stages of the transaction.

2. Dodd-Frank Act: This law was enacted to regulate mortgage lending practices and protect consumers from predatory practices. It has implications for wholesalers dealing with distressed properties or involved in financing arrangements.

3. Truth in Lending Act (TILA): TILA mandates lenders to disclose important information to borrowers, including interest rates and fees. While wholesalers are generally not subject to TILA, they should be aware of it as they often work closely with buyers who may need loans.

4. Fair Housing Act: The Fair Housing Act prohibits discrimination against protected classes in the sale, rental, and financing of properties. Wholesalers must avoid any discriminatory practices and treat all potential buyers fairly.

5. State and Local Regulations: Many states and cities have their own specific rules that govern real estate transactions. Wholesalers should familiarize themselves with these regulations as they can vary from one jurisdiction to another. In some cases, wholesalers may even need to obtain a real estate license to operate legally.

Importance of Compliance in the Wholesaling Business:

Compliance with laws and regulations is crucial for wholesalers to protect their business interests and maintain a positive reputation. Non-compliance can lead to severe consequences, such as substantial fines, property repossession, and even criminal charges. On the other hand, maintaining compliance builds trust and credibility within the industry, establishing wholesalers as reliable and trustworthy partners.

In conclusion, understanding the basics of real estate law and the relevant regulations affecting wholesaling is essential for success in this business. Adhering to these laws not only ensures legal compliance but also helps wholesalers to establish a strong reputation and long-term success in the industry.

When establishing a real estate wholesaling business, it is crucial to ensure that all legal requirements are met right from the start. This involves considering the appropriate business structure and fulfilling the necessary registrations and licensing.

Selecting the right business structure is a critical decision that should not be taken lightly. Various options exist, such as Limited Liability Company (LLC), S-Corporation, C-Corporation, and general partnerships. Each structure carries implications related to tax liability, personal liability, and governance. Many real estate wholesalers opt for LLCs due to their flexibility, pass-through taxation benefits, and liability protection.

To operate as a real estate wholesaler, it is important to comply with licensing and registration obligations. Depending on the jurisdiction, a real estate license may be required, particularly if your activities include connecting buyers and sellers of properties. Additionally, obtaining a business license is generally mandatory, ensuring that your business operates within the legal framework. This may involve acquiring permits specific to your location.

Furthermore, it is essential to obtain a Tax ID Number, such as an Employer Identification Number (EIN), for tax filing purposes and other financial obligations. If your wholesaling activities involve the purchase and resale of goods, such as furniture or appliances, you may need to obtain a seller's permit.

Keep in mind that additional permits and licenses may be necessary depending on the nature of your business and its location. These can include zoning permits, occupancy permits, or environmental permits. It is crucial to thoroughly research and understand the specific requirements in your area, as licensing and registration requirements can vary from one jurisdiction to another and may change over time.

By adhering to these regulations and requirements from the inception of your business, you can avoid potential legal issues and ensure a solid foundation for your real estate wholesaling endeavors. It is always recommended to consult with legal professionals or relevant authorities to obtain accurate and up-to-date information regarding compliance with the laws and regulations applicable to your specific business circumstances.

Establishing a legally compliant real estate wholesaling business involves meticulous planning and attention to detail. By following the necessary steps and fulfilling all requirements, you not only ensure your business's long-term success but also build a reputation for professionalism and trustworthiness within the industry.

Setting up your business legally begins with selecting the most suitable business structure. Each structure has its own advantages and considerations, and it is essential to evaluate them in the context of your specific business goals and objectives.

1. Limited Liability Company (LLC): An LLC is a popular choice for real estate wholesalers due to its flexible management structure and liability protection. It combines the benefits of a corporation and a partnership, offering limited liability to its members while allowing for pass-through taxation. Forming an LLC typically involves filing Articles of Organization and drafting an Operating Agreement.

2. S-Corporation: An S-Corporation is a type of corporation that provides liability protection and allows for pass-through taxation. To establish an S-Corporation, you must first form a standard corporation and then file Form 2553 with the Internal Revenue Service (IRS) to elect S-Corporation status. Keep in mind that S-Corporations have more stringent requirements regarding the number and eligibility of shareholders.

3. C-Corporation: A C-Corporation is a separate legal entity that offers limited liability to its shareholders. Unlike an S-Corporation, it does not have restrictions on the number and eligibility of shareholders. However, C-Corporations are subject to double taxation, as the corporation itself is taxed on its profits, and shareholders are also taxed on their dividends.

4. General Partnership: A general partnership is the simplest and most informal business structure. It involves two or more individuals engaging in a business together, with shared management responsibilities and unlimited personal liability. While a partnership agreement is not legally required, it is highly recommended to document the rights, responsibilities, and profit-sharing arrangements of each partner.

Once you have chosen the appropriate business structure, it is necessary to complete various registrations and obtain the required licenses to operate your real estate wholesaling business legally. The exact requirements may vary depending on your location, so it is important to familiarize yourself with the specific regulations in your jurisdiction.

1. Real Estate License: In some states or jurisdictions, real estate wholesalers may be required to hold a real estate license. This requirement typically applies if your activities involve finding buyers or sellers of real estate properties. To obtain a real estate license, you will need to complete the necessary pre-licensing courses, pass a licensing exam, and fulfill any additional requirements set by the licensing authority.

2. Business License: Most local governments require businesses to obtain a general business license. This license ensures that your business is operating within the legal framework established by the local authorities. The process of obtaining a business license varies depending on your location and the specific requirements of the issuing agency. It may involve submitting an application, paying a fee, and providing certain documents, such as proof of identity and proof of address.

3. Tax ID Number (EIN): An Employer Identification Number (EIN) is required for various tax-related purposes, including filing taxes, opening a business bank account, and hiring employees. Even if you

are a sole proprietorship without any employees, obtaining an EIN is recommended as it separates your business's tax obligations from your personal finances. You can apply for an EIN online through the IRS website.

4. Seller's Permit: If your real estate wholesaling activities involve the purchase and resale of goods or materials, you may need to obtain a seller's permit. This permit enables you to collect and remit sales tax on the goods you sell. The requirements to obtain a seller's permit vary by jurisdiction, but generally involve completing an application, providing certain business information, and potentially paying a fee.

5. Additional Permits and Licenses: Depending on your location and the nature of your real estate wholesaling business, there may be additional permits or licenses required. These might include zoning permits, occupancy permits, or environmental permits. Zoning permits ensure that your business activities comply with the local zoning regulations, while occupancy permits certify that your premises are safe and suitable for the intended use. Environmental permits might be necessary if your operations involve activities that could impact the environment.

It is crucial to thoroughly research and understand the specific licensing and registration requirements for real estate wholesalers in your area. Local government websites and business resource centers can provide valuable information and guidance regarding the necessary steps and documentation needed to complete the registration and licensing process.

Once all the necessary registrations and licenses have been obtained, it is essential to maintain compliance with the relevant laws and regulations governing your real estate wholesaling business. This includes fulfilling any ongoing reporting and renewal requirements, complying with tax obligations, and staying up-to-date with any changes in the legal and regulatory landscape.

Keeping accurate and organized records is crucial for maintaining legal compliance and demonstrating transparency in your business operations. It is recommended to consult with legal professionals, such as attorneys and accountants, who specialize in real estate and business law. They can provide personalized advice and guidance tailored to your specific circumstances, ensuring that your real estate wholesaling business operates legally and efficiently.

In conclusion, when establishing a real estate wholesaling business, it is imperative to set it up legally and comply with all necessary registrations and licensing requirements. This involves selecting an appropriate business structure and fulfilling obligations such as obtaining a real estate license, business license, Tax ID Number (EIN), and seller's permit. Additional permits and licenses may also be required, depending on the nature of your business and its location. By following these steps and seeking guidance from professionals, you can ensure that your real estate wholesaling business operates legally and paves the way for long-term success.

Understanding Disclosure Requirements:
In real estate transactions, disclosure requirements play a critical role in ensuring transparency and protecting the interests of all parties involved. When engaging in wholesale transactions, it is essential for real estate wholesalers to understand what needs to be disclosed. This includes providing complete and accurate information to the other party about various aspects of the property or transaction.

Key areas of disclosure often include material defects, environmental hazards, property history, and legal or financial obligations related to the property being wholesaled. Material defects refer to significant structural or functional issues that could affect the value or safety of the property, such as plumbing or electrical problems, roof leaks, or foundation issues. Environmental hazards may include the presence of lead-based paint, asbestos, mold, or other substances that could pose health risks or require remediation. Property history disclosures involve sharing information about any previous damages, insurance claims, renovations, or other relevant events that may impact the property's value or desirability.

Consequences of Non-Compliance:
Non-compliance with disclosure requirements in real estate transactions can lead to serious consequences for wholesalers. These consequences can include legal liabilities, potential lawsuits, financial penalties, and reputational damage. When wholesalers fail to disclose required information, it can result in allegations of fraud or misrepresentation, eroding trust in the transaction and damaging relationships with buyers or other parties involved.

In addition to legal and financial repercussions, non-compliance with disclosure requirements can also lead to the cancellation of the transaction. If the other party later discovers undisclosed defects or hazards, they may have legal recourse to terminate the contract or seek remedies. Moreover, failure to comply with disclosure obligations can harm a wholesaler's reputation in the industry, making it more difficult to conduct future business and establish trust with potential buyers or partners.

Therefore, understanding and adhering to disclosure requirements are of utmost importance for real estate wholesalers. By fulfilling these obligations, wholesalers can maintain ethical standards, ensure transparency in transactions, protect all parties involved, and foster a positive and trustworthy business environment.

Navigating Zoning Laws and Regulations and their Impact on Real Estate Wholesaling:

Zoning laws and regulations have a profound impact on real estate wholesaling activities. These laws dictate how properties can be used, the type of structures that can be built, and the overall development of a specific area. As a real estate wholesaler, it is essential to understand the various zoning requirements in your local area and how they can impact your transactions.

For example, if you are a wholesaler looking to purchase a property to resell it, you may need to ensure that the property is zoned for residential or commercial use, depending on the intended buyer. Failing to comply with zoning laws can result in legal liabilities, fines, and reputational damage that can harm future business prospects. Additionally, zoning laws can impact the overall demand and value of properties in a given area, which can affect real estate transactions.

Therefore, navigating zoning laws and regulations is critical to successful real estate wholesaling. Fortunately, there are different resources and methods available to help wholesalers understand and comply with local zoning ordinances.

How to Research and Comply with Local Zoning Ordinances:

If you are a real estate wholesaler, researching and complying with local zoning ordinances is a critical process that can impact the success of your transactions. Here are some steps that you can take to research and comply with local zoning ordinances:

1. Develop an understanding of zoning laws: Start by researching and understanding different zoning laws and regulations in your local area. Identify the various zoning requirements, restrictions, and processes that may impact your real estate transactions.

2. Check zoning maps to verify the property's zoning classification: Zoning maps are public records that outline the different zoning classifications of properties within a locality. Verify the property's zoning classification before engaging in real estate wholesaling transactions.

3. Check the zoning ordinance for the property's intended use: Each zoning classification requires specific uses and restrictions. Comprehend the zoning ordinance to ensure that a proposed use is allowed.

4. Comply with all zoning requirements and build codes: Zoning enforcement is an essential component of ensuring compliance with zoning laws. Failure to comply with zoning requirements and build codes can result in fines, legal liabilities, and reputational damage.

In summary, real estate wholesalers must have a strong understanding of local zoning laws and regulations. Compliance with these laws is essential to ensure successful real estate transactions and to avoid the legal, financial, and reputational consequences of non-compliance. Researching local zoning laws and regulations before engaging in transactions can help wholesalers identify potential compliance issues and take appropriate action.

Tax Implications and Management: Overview of Tax Responsibilities for Wholesalers

As a wholesaler, it is crucial to understand the tax implications and responsibilities that come with the business. By having a clear understanding of the tax obligations, wholesalers can ensure compliance with tax laws and optimize their tax planning and management strategies. Here are the key aspects to consider:

1. Business Entity Classification: Wholesalers should first determine their business entity classification, such as sole proprietorship, partnership, limited liability company (LLC), or corporation. Each entity type has different tax implications, so it is essential to select the most suitable structure for your business needs, considering factors like liability protection and tax benefits.

2. Tax Identification Numbers: Wholesalers must obtain the necessary tax identification numbers, such as an Employer Identification Number (EIN) from the Internal Revenue Service (IRS). This identification number is necessary for filing taxes, opening bank accounts, and performing other financial transactions related to the business.

3. Sales Tax Compliance: Wholesalers need to be aware of their sales tax obligations. Depending on the jurisdiction, wholesalers may be required to collect and remit sales tax on their transactions. It is crucial to understand the specific sales tax laws and regulations in the jurisdictions where you operate and ensure proper compliance to avoid penalties or legal issues.

4. Income Tax Reporting: Wholesalers must accurately report their business income and expenses to determine their taxable income. This includes maintaining detailed records of sales, purchases, and operating expenses. Depending on the business entity type, wholesalers may need to file specific tax forms, such as Schedule C (sole proprietorship) or Form 1065 (partnership).

5. L Estimated Tax Payments: Wholesalers are typically subject to quarterly estimated tax payments. These payments are made throughout the year to cover federal and state income taxes, ensuring that tax liabilities are met and potential penalties are avoided. Proper tax planning can help estimate the required quarterly tax payments and prevent any surprises during tax filing season.

6. Deductions and Credits: Wholesalers should be aware of the deductions and credits available to them. Common deductions include expenses related to the purchase, storage, and transportation of goods, as well as business-related expenses like marketing and office supplies. Taking advantage of these deductions can lower the overall tax liabilities for wholesalers.

Strategies for Efficient Tax Planning and Management:

Efficient tax planning and management can help wholesalers optimize their tax liabilities and ensure compliance with legal requirements. Consider the following strategies to enhance your tax planning and management:

1. Engage with a Tax Professional: Working with an experienced tax professional who specializes in small businesses or real estate can provide valuable guidance on tax planning and management strategies. They can help identify deductions, navigate complex tax laws, and ensure compliance with reporting requirements.

2. .Maintain Accurate Records: Keeping thorough and organized records of all financial transactions is crucial for accurate tax reporting. Use accounting software or consult an accountant to establish systems for record-keeping, tracking income, expenses, and pertinent tax information. This will save time and effort during tax preparation and minimize the risk of errors.

3. Regularly Review and Adjust Tax Strategies: Tax laws and regulations may change over time, and your business circumstances may also evolve. Regularly reviewing and adjusting your tax strategies can help you stay up to date with the latest tax provisions and take advantage of available opportunities for tax savings.

4. Incorporate Tax Planning in Business Decisions: When making significant business decisions, consider the tax implications associated with each option. For example, when acquiring new inventory or assets, evaluate the tax consequences and structure the transactions in a tax-efficient manner. Consulting with a tax advisor can help you make informed decisions that align with your business goals and minimize tax burdens.

5. Utilize Retirement Accounts and Health Savings Accounts (HSAs): Contributing to retirement accounts, such as Individual Retirement

Accounts (IRAs) or Simplified Employee Pension (SEP) IRAs, can provide tax advantages while helping you save for retirement. Additionally, Health Savings Accounts (HSAs) offer tax benefits for qualified medical expenses. Explore these options to take advantage of potential tax savings.

6. Stay Informed About Tax Law Changes: Tax laws and regulations can fluctuate, so it's essential to stay updated on any changes that may impact your business. Follow reliable sources of tax information and consider attending tax seminars or workshops to ensure you are aware of new developments that may affect your tax planning strategies.

In conclusion, wholesalers should proactively manage their tax implications and responsibilities by understanding their tax obligations, maintaining accurate records, and implementing effective tax planning strategies. By staying informed, seeking professional advice, and employing the appropriate tax management techniques, wholesalers can optimize their tax liabilities and ensure compliance with tax laws while focusing on their business growth and success.

Real Estate Wholesaling

Real estate wholesaling can be a lucrative business, but it also comes with potential legal risks and pitfalls. It is crucial to navigate the legal landscape carefully to ensure compliance with the law and protect your interests. Here are some common legal mistakes to avoid, along with tips for risk management and legal safety:

1. Understanding and Complying with State and Local Laws: Real estate laws can vary from state to state and even from city to city. Familiarize yourself with the specific laws and regulations governing real estate wholesaling in your area. Research licensing requirements, disclosure obligations, advertising restrictions, and any other legal obligations imposed by your jurisdiction.

2. Engaging in Unauthorized Practice of Law: Wholesalers should avoid providing legal advice or engaging in activities that require a license to practice law. Offering legal opinions or drafting legal documents can expose wholesalers to unauthorized practice of law claims. It is essential to work with competent legal professionals when it comes to legal matters.

3. Properly Documenting Transactions: Transactions in real estate wholesaling should be thoroughly documented to protect all parties involved. Use written contracts that clearly outline the terms and conditions of the transaction, including assignment clauses. Working with a qualified real estate attorney can help ensure the contracts are properly drafted and legally sound.

4. Transparent and Honest Communication: Maintaining transparent and honest communication with all parties involved in a transaction is crucial. This includes buyers, sellers, and other stakeholders. Disclose all relevant information, such as the assignment of the contract and any potential conflicts of interest. Honesty and transparency can help prevent legal disputes down the line.

5. Compliance with Advertising Regulations: When marketing wholesale properties, ensure compliance with advertising regulations. Avoid making false or misleading statements about a property or the transaction. Familiarize yourself with the rules surrounding advertising and ensure all advertisements are accurate and in compliance with local regulations.

6. Consult with Professionals: It is highly recommended to work with qualified professionals throughout the wholesaling process. This includes real estate attorneys, title companies, and experienced real estate agents who can provide guidance and ensure legal compliance. Consulting with professionals can help mitigate legal risks and navigate complex transactions.

7. Ongoing Education: Real estate laws and regulations are subject to changes and updates. Stay updated with changes in the law, attend seminars or workshops, and engage in ongoing education. Staying informed about legal requirements can help you adapt your practices and avoid legal pitfalls.

In conclusion, real estate wholesaling can be a rewarding venture, but it is crucial to navigate the legal landscape carefully. By understanding and complying with state and local laws, properly documenting transactions, maintaining open communication, and seeking guidance from professionals, you can minimize legal risks and ensure legal safety in your wholesaling business. Stay informed, adapt to changes in the law, and prioritize ethical business practices to build a successful and legally compliant wholesaling career.

Using Legal Counsel: When and How to Seek Legal Advice

Seeking legal advice is essential in various situations to protect your rights, interests, and ensure legal compliance. Here are some common scenarios where seeking legal counsel is recommended:

1. Starting a Business: When starting a business, legal advice can help you choose the right legal structure, such as a sole proprietorship, partnership, or corporation. An attorney can guide you through the process of registering your business, obtaining necessary licenses, and drafting contracts.

2. Contracts and Agreements: Before entering into any contracts or agreements, it's crucial to have a lawyer review the terms and conditions. Legal counsel can ensure that contracts are fair, protect your rights, and minimize legal risks. This includes business contracts, employment agreements, lease agreements, and more.

3. Intellectual Property Protection: If you have unique inventions, trademarks, copyrights, or trade secrets, seeking legal advice is critical for protecting your intellectual property rights. An attorney can help you apply for patents or trademarks, enforce intellectual property rights, and defend against infringement claims.

4. Employment Issues: When dealing with employment matters such as hiring, firing, discrimination claims, or disputes, legal counsel can provide guidance on labor laws, employee rights, and help navigate potential legal pitfalls.

5. Regulatory Compliance: In regulated industries, such as healthcare or finance, it is crucial to comply with specific laws and regulations. Legal advice can ensure that your business operates within the legal framework and avoids penalties or legal consequences.

6. Dispute Resolution: If you are involved in a legal dispute, seeking legal counsel is essential. An attorney can assess the situation, provide advice on potential legal remedies, negotiate settlements, or represent you in court.

7. Estate Planning: Legal advice is crucial when planning your estate, creating wills or trusts, or establishing power of attorney. An attorney can help ensure your assets are distributed according to your wishes and minimize potential disputes among beneficiaries.

When seeking legal advice, it's important to find the right attorney who specializes in the relevant area of law. Consider their experience, expertise, track record, and their ability to communicate effectively.

Benefits of Ongoing Legal Support

Having ongoing legal support can provide numerous benefits for individuals and businesses alike. Here are some advantages of establishing an ongoing relationship with legal counsel:

1. Preventing Legal Issues: By having a lawyer on retainer or establishing an ongoing relationship, you can proactively address legal matters. Your attorney can identify potential risks, provide advice on compliance, and help you avoid legal issues before they escalate.

2. Strategic Decision-Making: Legal counsel can provide valuable input and guidance during strategic decision-making processes. They can help you assess legal risks, advise on potential consequences, and offer solutions to protect your interests.

3. Drafting and Reviewing Legal Documents: Having ongoing legal support ensures that all your legal documents are properly drafted and reviewed. From contracts and agreements to company policies and procedures, your attorney can ensure that they are legally sound and protect your rights.

4. Compliance and Regulatory Support: In regulated industries, ongoing legal counsel can help navigate the complex maze of laws and regulations. They can assist with compliance audits, develop internal policies, and ensure adherence to industry-specific regulations.

5. Dispute Resolution and Litigation: If a legal dispute arises, having a lawyer already familiar with your business can save time and help resolve the issue more efficiently. Your attorney can guide you through negotiation, mediation, or represent you in court if necessary.

6. Cost-Effective Approach: While legal services come at a cost, having ongoing legal support can be a cost-effective approach in the long run. By identifying and addressing legal issues proactively, you can prevent costly litigation and potential legal consequences.

7. Peace of Mind: Perhaps the most significant benefit of ongoing legal support is the peace of mind it provides. Knowing that you have a trusted legal advisor available to guide you through legal complexities can alleviate stress and allow you to focus on your core business activities.

In conclusion, seeking legal counsel is crucial in various situations to protect your rights, interests, and ensure legal compliance. Whether you need legal advice for specific situations or establish ongoing legal support, having a trusted attorney by your side can provide numerous benefits. By understanding when and how to seek legal advice and the advantages of ongoing legal support, you can navigate legal complexities with confidence and protect your personal or business interests effectively.

Part II: Launching Your Business

Entrepreneurship is a thrilling journey filled with challenges and opportunities, and launching a business is a pivotal moment that requires careful planning and strategic execution. In the ever-evolving world of real estate wholesaling, "The 7 Figure Blueprint" serves as an invaluable guide for individuals looking to establish a successful and lucrative venture in this industry.

This comprehensive book takes readers on a step-by-step journey, providing them with a roadmap to navigate the intricate process of building a thriving real estate wholesaling business. It demystifies the complexities of this field while equipping aspiring entrepreneurs with the knowledge, skills, and confidence needed to achieve substantial financial success.

"The 7 Figure Blueprint" starts by establishing a strong foundation, offering insights into the fundamentals of real estate wholesaling. From understanding the market dynamics and identifying profitable investment opportunities to developing a robust business model, readers are guided through each crucial aspect of the process. This book emphasizes the significance of meticulous market research and effective networking strategies to establish valuable connections within the industry.

Further chapters delve into the formulation of a winning marketing strategy, exploring various channels such as digital marketing, social media platforms, and offline promotional activities. Practical tips and techniques are shared to help readers effectively reach their target audience, generate leads, and secure profitable deals. Additionally, the book highlights the importance of building a reputable brand presence and cultivating a strong professional network to grow and expand the business.

"The 7 Figure Blueprint" goes beyond theoretical knowledge, providing actionable advice on negotiating deals, conducting thorough due diligence, and closing transactions successfully. It also offers valuable insights into managing risk, creating optimal financial structures, and maximizing profitability in real estate wholesaling.

What sets "The 7 Figure Blueprint" apart is its emphasis on scalability and long-term sustainability. The author shares valuable lessons learned from personal experiences, highlighting potential pitfalls and offering guidance to avoid common mistakes. Through detailed case studies and real-life examples, readers gain a deeper understanding of the challenges they may encounter and how to overcome them.

"The 7 Figure Blueprint: A Step-by-Step Field Manual for Building a Real Estate Wholesaling Business" is an essential resource for aspiring entrepreneurs seeking to launch their own real estate wholesaling ventures. With its comprehensive approach, practical insights, and actionable strategies, this book empowers readers to embark on their entrepreneurial journey armed with the knowledge and tools needed to achieve substantial success in the dynamic world of real estate wholesaling.

Chapter 3: Setting Up Your Business Structure

Business entities are fundamental building blocks of the corporate world, providing the legal framework for conducting various commercial activities. Understanding different types of business entities is crucial for entrepreneurs and business owners as it directly impacts the structure, operations, taxation, and liabilities of their ventures. In this comprehensive guide, we will explore the main types of business entities, namely Sole Proprietorship, Partnership, Corporation, and Limited Liability Company (LLC), along with the important factors to consider when choosing the most suitable business structure.

Sole Proprietorship:
A sole proprietorship is the simplest and most common form of business entity where an individual operates a business on their own. In this structure, the owner has complete control over the business and is responsible for all its profits, losses, and liabilities. While it offers simplicity and autonomy, sole proprietorships also come with unlimited personal liability and potential challenges in raising capital.

Partnership:
Partnerships involve two or more individuals who share ownership and responsibility for a business. There are different types of partnerships, including general partnerships, limited partnerships, and limited liability partnerships (LLPs). Partnerships offer shared decision-making, shared profits, and shared liabilities. It is crucial for partners to clearly define their roles and responsibilities and have a well-drafted partnership agreement to avoid conflicts and potential legal issues.

Corporation:
A corporation is a separate legal entity from its owners, known as shareholders. The corporation offers limited liability protection to shareholders, meaning their personal assets are generally shielded from the company's debts and liabilities. Corporations have more complex structures, including a board of directors, officers, and shareholders. They often have more flexibility in raising capital through the issuance of stocks, but also have additional compliance requirements and are subject to double taxation on profits.

Limited Liability Company (LLC):
LLCs offer a hybrid structure, combining the benefits of both partnerships and corporations. They provide limited liability protection to owners (called

members) while maintaining flexibility in management and taxation. LLCs are relatively easy to set up and maintain compared to corporations, making them a popular choice for small to medium-sized businesses. However, the specific regulations governing LLCs can vary by jurisdiction.

Factors to Consider When Choosing a Business Structure:
Selecting the most suitable business structure requires careful consideration of various factors. Key considerations include:
1. Liability Protection: Assessing the level of personal liability protection needed to safeguard personal assets from business debts and legal claims.
2. Tax Implications: Analyzing the tax obligations, advantages, and disadvantages associated with different business structures, such as pass-through taxation or corporate tax rates.
3. Management Flexibility: Determining the desired level of autonomy and decision-making authority in the business's management structure.
4. Ease of Formation: Evaluating the complexity and costs involved in establishing and maintaining different business structures, including compliance requirements.
5. Future Growth and Exit Strategy: Considering the potential growth trajectory of the business and the flexibility to bring in investors or exit the business when desired.

Conclusion:
Choosing the right business entity is a critical decision that can impact the success, profitability, and legal obligations of a business venture. Understanding the characteristics, advantages, and disadvantages of sole proprietorships, partnerships, corporations, and LLCs is crucial for making an informed choice. Additionally, evaluating factors such as liability protection, tax implications, management flexibility, ease of formation, and future growth plans will help entrepreneurs select the most suitable business structure that aligns with their goals and aspirations.

Please note that the word count may vary slightly based on formatting and specific content requirements.

A Sole Proprietorship is a common business structure for real estate wholesalers, where an individual operates their wholesale business as the sole owner. It is a straightforward and affordable option to start and run a business with complete control over its operations.

Real estate wholesalers who choose a sole proprietorship have some unique characteristics. They have complete control over their business decisions and operations, including marketing, finding deals, negotiating contracts, and managing finances. This autonomy allows them to capitalize on their strengths and respond quickly to market trends. Sole proprietors do not have to adhere to any partnership or shareholder agreements and they can set their own policies and procedures for the business.

Pros of Sole Proprietorship for Real Estate Wholesalers:
The sole proprietorship structure has several advantages for real estate wholesalers. Firstly, it is relatively easy and affordable to set up with no requirements for legal formalities such as filing articles of organization or annual reports. This saves legal fees and time, allowing wholesalers to focus on growing their business. Secondly, a sole proprietorship provides full control and decision-making power to the owner without having to share any profits with partners or shareholders. This means that the wholesaler can make decisions based on their expertise and intuition, achieving more significant financial gains.

Cons of Sole Proprietorship for Real Estate Wholesalers:
One major disadvantage of a Sole Proprietorship is unlimited personal liability. As a sole owner, the wholesaler is personally liable for all debts, liabilities, and legal issues incurred by the business. This means that creditors and litigants can go after the wholesaler's personal assets to pay off any liability incurred by the business. Therefore, obtaining appropriate insurance and implementing risk management strategies is crucial. Additionally, a sole proprietor may face issues in raising capital and obtaining loans, especially without a track record or positive financial history.

In summary, a sole proprietorship can be a viable option for real estate wholesalers due to its simplicity, autonomy, and affordability. However, they should weigh the benefits and drawbacks of this structure, especially the unlimited liability that comes with it, and consider consulting with legal or financial experts to weigh their options effectively. Real estate wholesalers should continuously assess their business needs and goals regularly and may switch to alternative business structures like LLCs or S-Corporations as they expand or encounter new challenges.

Remember, this is not legal or financial advice, this is informational content only. Entrepreneurs should consult with qualified professionals before making any business decisions.

Partnerships are a common business structure wherein two or more individuals agree to work together with the aim of achieving mutual benefits. It is a flexible type of business structure with more than one owner sharing ownership, profits, and losses. There are two main types of partnerships – general and limited.

General Partnership:
A general partnership is the most common type of partnership. In this structure, each partner is jointly and severally liable for the partnership's debts and obligations. All partners share unlimited liability, which means they can be personally responsible for business losses, debts, or legal matters that arise. Additionally, partners share in the profits, decision-making and participate in all aspects of the business. Each partner has equal power and authority, and all partners are equally responsible for the management of the company's operations.

Limited Partnership:
A limited partnership differs from a general partnership, as it consists of two types of partners, general and limited. In this structure, the general partners

are personally liable for all business obligations and debts, while limited partners are not. The limited partners are passive investors, who contribute capital to the business but do not engage in day-to-day operations. Consequently, limited partners have limited liability, which means that they are only liable for the amount of capital they invested. General partners make all the business decisions, manage the business, and have unlimited liability for all obligations and debts.

Legal and Financial Implications for Partners:
Partnerships, whether general or limited, have a significant legal and financial implications for the partners involved. Partnerships are not legal entities, therefore, each partner is held accountable for their actions regarding the business. All partners should work closely together, maintain transparent communication, and document their responsibilities and obligations through a written partnership agreement.

Some of the critical implications and responsibilities include the following:

- Liabilities: Partnerships have unlimited liability, meaning partners' personal assets can be used to settle the company's debts or legal issues. Partnerships require comprehensive risk management strategies and the right insurance coverage to minimize exposure.
- Taxes: Partnerships do not pay taxes directly; instead, each partner reports their share of the income or losses on their individual tax returns annually.
- Capital Contributions and Distributions: Each partner's capital contribution and distribution share should be proportionate to their ownership percentage, as specified in the partnership agreement.
- Decision-making: Partners must make financial and operational decisions collectively, as outlined in the partnership agreement.
- Dissolution: Partnerships are not permanent and can be dissolved by different triggers such as bankruptcy, death, or the expiration of the partnership agreement.

In conclusion, partnerships can be an effective business structure for entrepreneurs looking to minimize start-up costs and use their combined resources. General Partnerships and Limited Partnerships are two types of partnerships available to businesses, each with its own advantages and disadvantages. Partners should be aware of the legal and financial implications of partnerships, work closely together, establish clear responsibilities and obligations in writing and consult with professionals before making any substantial business decisions.

A Limited Liability Company (LLC) is a type of business structure that offers a combination of liability protection and flexible management options. It is considered a hybrid entity, combining some of the characteristics of a corporation and a partnership. LLCs offer a host of benefits for real estate wholesalers, including liability protection, flexibility, and various tax benefits.

Benefits of an LLC for Real Estate Wholesaling:

1. Limited Liability Protection: One of the most significant benefits of having an LLC is that it offers limited liability protection. This means that the business owners would not be personally liable for any debts or legal issues incurred by the business. Their personal assets would be shielded from business liabilities, which is essential as real estate wholesaling can be a high-risk business.

2. Flexible Management Structure: Unlike corporations, LLCs offer more flexibility in management structure. LLCs can be managed by either the owners or a third party. The owners can make decisions about who will manage the LLC without involving shareholders or a board of directors.

3. No Personal Income Tax: Income earned by the LLC is passed through directly to the owners, and each owner reports their share of the income on their personal tax returns. This avoids double taxation on income earned by the LLC.

4. Greater Business Credibility: LLCs provide greater credibility and professionalism, which can be beneficial in real estate wholesaling. LLCs are viewed as more professional and established than sole proprietorships, which can help secure more deals and repeat business.

Process of Forming and Maintaining an LLC:

1. Choose a Business Name: The first step in forming an LLC is to choose a name and make sure it's available in the state where you'll register the business.

2. File Articles of Organization: The Articles of Organization is a legal document that establishes the LLC's existence in the state where the business operates.

3. Draft an Operating Agreement: An operating agreement is a legal document that outlines how the LLC will be managed and the rights and responsibilities of each member. It is not a legal requirement in all states, but it is a crucial element in ensuring smooth business operations.

4. Obtain Business Licenses and Permits: Depending on the state and local regulations, LLCs may need specific business licenses

Corporations, specifically S-Corporations (S-Corps) and C-Corporations (C-Corps), are two distinct business structures with different characteristics, taxation methods, and liability considerations. Let's explore the differences between S-Corps and C-Corps, as well as the taxation and liability considerations associated with each.

1. S-Corporation (S-Corp):

- Pass-Through Taxation: One key feature of S-Corps is pass-through taxation. This means that the corporation itself does not pay income taxes. Instead, the profits and losses of the S-Corp "pass through" to the individual shareholders, who report them on their personal tax returns. This avoids the issue of double taxation that is common with C-Corps.

- Limited Liability Protection: Like C-Corps, S-Corps offer limited liability protection. This means that shareholders' personal assets are generally protected from the debts and liabilities of the corporation. However, it's important to note that personal guarantees or misconduct can potentially expose shareholders to personal liability.

- Ownership and Restrictions: S-Corps have restrictions on ownership. They must have domestic shareholders (US citizens or residents) and can have a maximum of 100 shareholders. S-Corps cannot have non-individual shareholders or foreign shareholders.

- Formalities and Regulations: S-Corps have specific requirements regarding corporate governance, such as holding regular meetings, maintaining corporate bylaws, and documenting major business decisions.

2. C-Corporation (C-Corp):

- Double Taxation: Unlike S-Corps, C-Corporations are subject to double taxation. This means that the corporation pays taxes on its profits at the corporate tax rate, and then shareholders are taxed on any dividends or distributions received from the corporation on their personal tax returns. This can result in higher overall tax liability.
- Unlimited Ownership and Shares: C-Corps have no restrictions on ownership or the number of shareholders. They can have both

individual and corporate shareholders and may issue multiple classes of shares.
- Formalities and Regulations: C-Corps generally have more formalities and regulatory requirements compared to S-Corps. This includes holding regular shareholder and board of directors meetings, recording meeting minutes, and adhering to specific corporate governance standards.

Taxation and Liability Considerations:

- S-Corps: The pass-through taxation of S-Corps allows for potentially lower tax rates and the ability to avoid double taxation. Shareholders report their share of the profits and losses on their personal tax returns. Additionally, S-Corps generally offer limited liability protection for shareholders, shielding their personal assets from business debts and liabilities.

- C-Corps: C-Corps are subject to double taxation as the corporation itself is taxed on its profits, while shareholders are taxed on any dividends received. However, C-Corps may offer certain tax advantages, such as deductible employee benefits and more flexibility in structuring compensation. C-Corps also provide limited liability protection to shareholders.

When choosing between an S-Corp and C-Corp, it's crucial to consider the specific tax and liability implications that align with your business goals, the number and type of shareholders, and the desired level of formality and regulatory compliance.

It's important to consult with legal, tax, and financial professionals to determine which corporate structure best suits your needs and complies with the regulations in your jurisdiction. They can provide personalized guidance based on your specific circumstances and objectives.

Comparative analysis of different entity types, including a side-by-side comparison of liability, taxation, and operational considerations. This analysis can help you choose the right structure based on your business goals and scale.

1. Sole Proprietorship:
   - Liability: Sole proprietorship offers no separation between the business and the owner. This means the owner has unlimited personal liability for business debts and liabilities.
   - Taxation: As a sole proprietorship, business income and expenses are reported on the owner's personal tax return. It is subject to personal income tax rates.
   - Operational Considerations: Sole proprietorships are easy to set up, require minimal paperwork, and offer full control to the owner. However, funding options may be limited, and the business's scalability can be challenging.

2. Partnership:
   - Liability: In a general partnership, partners share unlimited personal liability for the business's debts and obligations. Limited partnerships offer limited liability protection to some partners.
   - Taxation: Partnerships file an informational tax return, but the business itself does not pay taxes. Instead, profits and losses pass through to the partners, who report them on their personal tax returns.
   - Operational Considerations: Partnerships benefit from shared decision-making, resources, and expertise. However, partnerships require a partnership agreement and may face challenges in terms of ownership changes and operational continuity.

3. Limited Liability Company (LLC):
   - Liability: LLCs provide limited liability protection to their owners (called members), separating personal assets from business debts and liabilities.

- Taxation: LLCs have flexibility in taxation. By default, they are taxed as pass-through entities, similar to partnerships. However, they can choose to be taxed as a corporation, either as an S-Corp or C-Corp, providing potential tax advantages.
- Operational Considerations: LLCs offer a balance between ease of operation and liability protection. They have fewer formalities compared to corporations but still require proper documentation, such as the operating agreement.

4. Corporation (C-Corp):
   - Liability: C-Corps provide limited liability protection to shareholders, allowing separation of personal assets from corporate debts and liabilities.
   - Taxation: C-Corps are subject to double taxation. The corporation pays taxes on profits, and shareholders pay taxes on dividends received from the corporation.
   - Operational Considerations: Corporations are well-suited for large-scale operations, raising capital through the sale of stock, and attracting potential investors. However, they have more formalities, such as shareholder meetings, maintaining corporate bylaws, and issuing stock certificates.

Choosing the right structure:

- Consider Liability Protection: If protecting personal assets is a priority, forming an LLC or corporation generally offers better liability protection compared to sole proprietorships or partnerships.
- Evaluate Tax Implications: Assess the tax advantages and disadvantages of each entity type. Pass-through taxation can be

beneficial for some businesses, while others may find the corporate tax structure more advantageous.

- Assess Operational Needs: Consider the level of flexibility, decision-making structure, compliance requirements, and scalability needed for your business. Each entity type has different operational considerations that may impact daily operations, ownership changes, and growth potential.

- Seek Professional Guidance: Consulting with legal, tax, and financial professionals is crucial for making an informed decision. They can provide personalized advice based on your specific business goals, scale, industry, and jurisdiction.

Remember, each business is unique, and there is no one-size-fits-all solution. Carefully evaluate the liability, taxation, and operational aspects of each entity type to choose the structure that aligns best with your business goals and long-term vision.

The steps to legally register your business entity and the necessary documentation required for the registration process. Please note that the specific requirements and processes may vary depending on your jurisdiction. It's advisable to consult with a legal professional or local business registration authority to ensure compliance with local laws and regulations.

1. Choose a Business Name:
   - Select a unique and suitable name for your business that complies with the naming regulations of your jurisdiction.
   - Conduct a name availability search or reservation if required.

2. Determine the Business Structure:
   - Decide on the type of business entity, such as sole proprietorship, partnership, LLC, or corporation, based on your specific needs, liability considerations, and tax implications.

3. Obtain the Necessary Licenses and Permits:
   - Research and obtain any licenses, permits, or registrations required for your specific industry or location. This may include general business licenses, professional licenses, health permits, and more.

4. Prepare and File the Required Documentation:
   - Complete the appropriate registration forms and prepare the necessary documentation according to your chosen business structure.

Sole Proprietorship:
   - Typically, no formal registration is required. However, you may need to file a "Doing Business As" (DBA) or fictitious name registration if you operate under a name different from your legal name.

Partnership:
   - Prepare a partnership agreement outlining the terms and conditions of the partnership.
   - Register the partnership with the appropriate local or state authority, including filing the necessary partnership registration forms.

Limited Liability Company (LLC):
   - Prepare and file Articles of Organization or Certificate of Formation, depending on your jurisdiction.
   - Draft an Operating Agreement that outlines the management structure and internal operations of the LLC.

Corporation:
   - Prepare and file Articles of Incorporation, typically including details such as the company name, purpose, share structure, and registered agent information.
   - Create corporate bylaws that establish the rules and regulations for the corporation's operation and governance.

5. Pay the Required Fees:
   - Be prepared to pay the necessary registration and filing fees associated with your business structure and jurisdiction. The fees may vary depending on the type of entity and location.

6. Register for Taxes:
   - Obtain an Employer Identification Number (EIN) from the relevant tax authority, such as the Internal Revenue Service (IRS) in the United States. This is required for most businesses, even if you do not have employees.

7. File Registration with the Appropriate Authorities:
   - Submit the completed registration forms and supporting documents to the relevant local, state, or federal government agency responsible for business registrations.

8. Obtain any Additional Approvals or Registrations:
   - Depending on your industry, you may need to seek additional approvals or registrations with specific regulatory bodies. Examples include environmental permits, health and safety certifications, or professional licenses.

9. Periodic Renewal and Compliance:

   - Be aware of any renewal requirements or ongoing compliance obligations, such as annual reports, tax filings, or maintaining proper business records. Stay updated on changes in regulations or reporting requirements to ensure ongoing compliance.

It's important to keep in mind that the registration process can be complex and time-consuming. Seeking legal advice or consulting with a business registration professional can help ensure that you complete all necessary steps accurately and efficiently.

When it comes to real estate wholesaling, obtaining the necessary licenses and permits can vary depending on your jurisdiction. To ensure compliance, here are some general steps to consider:

1. Research Licensing Requirements:
   - Understand the licensing requirements specific to real estate wholesaling in your area. Check with your local real estate commission or regulatory agency to determine the necessary licenses and permits.

2. Consult with Legal Professionals:
   - Seek guidance from a real estate attorney or legal professional well-versed in real estate laws and regulations in your jurisdiction.
   - They can provide tailored advice and ensure that you comply with all legal requirements.

3. Obtain a Real Estate License (if required):
   - Determine if obtaining a real estate license is necessary for engaging in wholesaling activities in your area.
   - If required, complete the necessary education, training, and licensing exams to obtain your real estate license.

4. Business Registration and Permits:
   - Register your business entity with the appropriate local authorities, obtaining any general business licenses or permits that may be required.
   - Check with your city or county government to determine the specific permits needed for wholesaling real estate.

5. Stay Informed and Compliant:
   - Keep yourself up to date with any changes in federal, state, or local laws related to real estate wholesaling.
   - Maintain compliance with regulations, including fair housing laws, disclosure requirements, and any specific rules or regulations governing wholesaling in your jurisdiction.

Remember, while these steps provide a general overview, it's important to consult with legal professionals or local regulatory agencies to ensure you follow the specific requirements in your area. They can provide you with accurate and up-to-date information on obtaining the necessary licenses and permits for real estate wholesaling in your jurisdiction.

Conclusion:

In conclusion, setting up your business structure is a crucial step when starting your real estate wholesaling venture. Selecting the right business structure can have significant implications for your business's liability, taxes, and overall operations. By carefully considering the options available and consulting with legal and financial professionals, you can choose a structure that best aligns with your goals and provides the necessary legal protection.

Summary of Key Points on Selecting and Setting Up a Business Structure:

1. Understand the different business structures available, such as sole proprietorship, partnership, limited liability company (LLC), and corporation.
2. Consider factors like liability protection, tax implications, ownership and management structure, and ease of operation when selecting a business structure.
3. Seek professional guidance from attorneys, accountants, or business advisors to assess your specific needs and determine the most suitable structure.
4. Follow the necessary legal requirements and register your business entity with the appropriate authorities.
5. Keep in mind that the chosen business structure can be modified or changed as your business grows and develops.

Brief Transition to the Importance of Effective Business Planning and Operation:

While selecting and setting up a business structure is crucial, it is equally important to have a comprehensive business plan and strategy in place. Effective business planning helps you outline your goals, target market, marketing strategies, financial projections, and operational procedures. It serves as a roadmap for success and allows you to make informed decisions while navigating the real estate wholesaling industry.

Moreover, efficient business operation is key to sustain and grow your wholesaling business. This includes managing finances, implementing marketing and sales strategies, building a network of potential buyers and sellers, and staying updated on the market trends and regulations. By focusing on effective business planning and operation, you can maximize your chances of success and achieve your desired outcomes in the real estate wholesaling sector.

Remember, starting a real estate wholesaling business requires careful consideration of both the business structure and effective planning and operation. Seek professional advice, stay informed, and adapt to the ever-changing dynamics of the real estate industry to thrive in your venture.

Chapter 4: Tools and Technology for Effective Operations

Introduction to Business Technology:
Importance of Leveraging Technology in Real Estate Wholesaling

In today's rapidly evolving business landscape, technology plays a pivotal role in transforming various industries, including real estate wholesaling. The advent of advanced tools and technology has revolutionized the way businesses operate, allowing them to streamline their operations, enhance efficiency, and achieve unprecedented levels of success. This chapter delves into the significance of leveraging technology in the realm of real estate wholesaling, providing an overview of how technology can streamline operations and increase efficiency in this dynamic industry.

The exponential growth and widespread adoption of technology have redefined the way businesses function across all sectors. Real estate wholesaling, which involves connecting motivated sellers with buyers, is no exception. By embracing innovative tools and harnessing the power of technology, wholesalers can elevate their operations, gain a competitive edge, and thrive in a highly competitive market.

One of the key benefits of adopting technology in real estate wholesaling is the ability to streamline operations. Traditional methods often involve labor-intensive and time-consuming tasks such as manual paperwork, data entry, and communication. However, with the right technology in place, wholesalers can automate these processes, reducing human error and freeing up valuable time to focus on more strategic activities.

Technology enables wholesalers to efficiently manage their leads, contacts, and deals through robust customer relationship management (CRM) software. This type of software allows wholesalers to organize and track interactions with sellers, buyers, and other stakeholders, facilitating effective communication and seamless collaboration. Additionally, CRM software offers features such as lead management, deal tracking, and analytics, providing valuable insights that inform decision-making and improve overall operational efficiency.

Another major advantage of technology in real estate wholesaling is the ability to streamline marketing efforts. With the help of digital platforms, wholesalers can reach a wider audience, generate leads, and initiate targeted marketing campaigns. Social media platforms, search engine optimization (SEO), and online advertising offer powerful avenues to showcase deals, attract potential buyers, and build a strong online presence. Additionally, virtual tours, high-quality images, and video walkthroughs can be utilized to provide an immersive and engaging experience for buyers. Harnessing these digital marketing strategies can result in increased visibility, accelerated deal flow, and ultimately, improved profitability.

Moreover, technology empowers wholesalers with accurate and up-to-date market data and analytics. Real estate market analysis tools provide comprehensive insights into trends, property values, and demand patterns, allowing wholesalers to make informed decisions. By studying historic data, market projections, and comparable sales, wholesalers can pinpoint lucrative investment opportunities, assess property values, and negotiate favorable deals. Empowered with data-backed knowledge, wholesalers can confidently navigate the complex real estate market and make strategic decisions that maximize profitability.

Furthermore, technology enables wholesalers to leverage automation and artificial intelligence (AI) to optimize their operations. AI-powered tools can automate repetitive tasks, such as lead generation, data entry, and email communication, reducing manual effort and enabling wholesalers to focus on high-value activities. Chatbots and virtual assistants can provide instant responses to inquiries, schedule appointments, and provide personalized assistance, enhancing customer service and creating a seamless experience for clients. By embracing automation and AI, wholesalers can enhance productivity, improve customer satisfaction, and scale their businesses more efficiently.

In conclusion, the rapid advancement of technology has ushered in a new era for real estate wholesaling. By embracing innovative tools and leveraging technology, wholesalers can streamline their operations, increase efficiency, and unlock new opportunities in this dynamic industry. The importance of technology in real estate wholesaling cannot be overstated. From automating processes and streamlining marketing efforts to providing accurate market data and enabling AI-powered optimization, technology empowers wholesalers to stay ahead of the curve and achieve remarkable success. As technology continues to evolve, wholesalers who embrace its potential will undoubtedly realize tremendous benefits, both in terms of operational efficiency and overall business growth.

Benefits of Using a CRM for Managing Contacts and Leads

In the realm of real estate wholesaling, managing contacts and leads efficiently is crucial for success. This is where Customer Relationship Management (CRM) systems come into play. A CRM system is a powerful tool that enables wholesalers to organize, track, and nurture their contacts and leads effectively. In this section, we will explore the benefits of using a CRM system in the context of real estate wholesaling.

One of the primary advantages of using a CRM system is improved organization and centralization of contact information. Wholesalers deal with a myriad of contacts, including motivated sellers, buyers, investors, and other industry professionals. With a CRM in place, wholesalers can store all contact information in a centralized database, making it easily accessible and searchable. This eliminates the need for manual entry or separate contact management systems, reducing the chances of errors and ensuring that no valuable information falls through the cracks.

CRM systems also offer features that enable wholesalers to track and manage leads effectively. Wholesaling relies heavily on lead generation, and a CRM can streamline this process. By integrating lead capture forms on websites or landing pages, wholesalers can automatically feed new leads into the CRM system. This eliminates the need for manual data entry and ensures that every lead is captured and logged efficiently. Additionally, CRM systems offer lead tracking capabilities, allowing wholesalers to monitor the progress of leads, track interactions, and analyze conversion rates. This valuable insight can help wholesalers identify the most promising leads and allocate resources strategically.

Another benefit of using a CRM system is improved communication and collaboration. Wholesaling involves maintaining regular contact with various stakeholders, including sellers, buyers, and other team members. CRM systems provide communication management features such as email integration, task management, and notifications. This ensures that all communication is centralized, timely, and organized, minimizing the chances of important messages being missed or forgotten. Additionally, CRM systems allow for collaboration within the team, enabling sharing of notes, updates, and documents related to specific leads or deals. This promotes efficient teamwork, enhances communication, and ultimately improves overall productivity.

Furthermore, CRM systems provide automation capabilities that save wholesalers significant time and effort. Task automation, such as setting reminders, scheduling follow-ups, or triggering email sequences, eliminates the need for manual repetitive tasks. Wholesalers can set up workflows or automation rules within the CRM system, ensuring that specific actions or notifications are triggered based on predefined criteria. This allows wholesalers to focus on high-value activities, such as negotiating deals or building relationships, while the CRM system handles routine tasks in the background.

When selecting a CRM system for real estate wholesaling, certain features are crucial to consider. Firstly, integration capabilities are essential. A CRM that can integrate with other real estate tools, such as marketing automation platforms, document management systems, or lead generation tools, can create a seamless workflow and enhance overall efficiency. Additionally, customization options are important as wholesalers have specific requirements and workflows. A CRM that allows customization of fields, layouts, and processes can adapt to the unique needs of a wholesaling business.

Choosing the right CRM tool for real estate wholesaling can seem overwhelming considering the plethora of options available. However, some industry-leading CRM systems are tailored specifically for real estate professionals. Here are a few recommended CRM tools for real estate wholesalers:

1. HubSpot CRM: HubSpot CRM offers a free and user-friendly solution that allows wholesalers to organize contacts, track deals, and automate tasks. It integrates well with other HubSpot tools, such as marketing automation and sales tools, providing a comprehensive ecosystem for wholesaling needs.

2. Salesforce: Salesforce is a highly customizable and robust CRM platform. It offers extensive features, including lead tracking, email integration, workflow automation, and analytics. Salesforce also provides industry-specific solutions and can be tailored to suit real estate wholesaling requirements.

3. Zoho CRM: Zoho CRM is a feature-rich solution that caters to businesses of all sizes. It offers lead management, automation, email integration, and analytics capabilities. Zoho CRM provides a comprehensive set of tools to streamline wholesaling operations effectively.

In conclusion, utilizing a CRM system in real estate wholesaling brings numerous benefits. From improved organization and centralization of contact information to efficient lead management, streamlined communication, and automation capabilities, CRM systems empower wholesalers to achieve greater productivity and success. By considering features such as integration capabilities and customization options, wholesalers can select the right CRM tool that aligns with their unique business needs. Recommended CRM tools such as HubSpot CRM, Salesforce, and Zoho CRM provide reliable solutions specifically tailored for real estate wholesaling, enabling wholesalers to streamline their operations and drive growth in this competitive industry.

Tools for Assessing Property Values, Market Trends, and Investment Viability

Real estate wholesaling involves making informed investment decisions based on accurate and up-to-date information about property values, market trends, and investment viability. To achieve this, wholesalers must utilize property and market analysis tools that enable them to assess the value of properties, analyze market trends, and evaluate investment opportunities effectively. This chapter discusses the various tools available to wholesalers for property and market analysis and how they can be used to make informed investment decisions.

One of the most common and traditional tools for assessing property values is the Comparative Market Analysis (CMA). A CMA provides wholesalers with estimates of property values based on recent sales of comparable properties in the same location. A CMA involves reviewing data on recently sold properties, analyzing their features that impact property value, such as size, age, location, and amenities, and comparing them to the subject property. This allows wholesalers to estimate an accurate range of price for the property, providing valuable information for negotiations and pricing decisions.

Another property analysis tool is the property inspector's report. This tool is used to evaluate the physical condition of the property, identifying any faulty systems, code violations, or safety risks that may impact the value of the property. Property inspectors assess the structural integrity, mechanical systems, and overall condition of the property, providing a comprehensive report that wholesalers can use to make informed investment decisions.

In addition to individual property analysis, wholesalers must also analyze market trends to evaluate investment opportunities accurately. Various market analysis tools are available to provide wholesalers with insights into average home prices, demand for real estate, and price trends. One such tool is the Multiple Listing Service (MLS), a platform used by real estate professionals to share property listings and track market trends. MLS data provides wholesalers with comprehensive information on property listings, sales data, and public records, allowing them to analyze competing properties and adjust their market strategies accordingly.

Investment viability analysis tools enable wholesalers to understand an investment's potential returns, risks, and cash flow. The net operating income (NOI) is one such tool that wholesalers can use to evaluate the profitability of an investment property. To calculate the NOI, wholesalers must subtract all operating expenses from the property's annual rental income. This provides wholesalers with a clear picture of the property's cash flow and profitability potential.

Real estate wholesalers can also use online market analysis tools such as Zillow, Redfin, and Trulia to gather data on property values, market trends, and investment opportunities. These tools offer real-time updates, providing wholesalers with current information on new listings, price changes, and foreclosures. Additionally, these platforms provide analytics on property values, rental rates, and other market trends, giving wholesalers valuable insights to make informed investment decisions.

To make informed investment decisions using these property and market analysis tools, wholesalers must know how to interpret and analyze the data effectively. This requires a thorough understanding of the local real estate market, valuation methodologies, and investment strategies. Wholesalers must also consider external factors such as economic and political trends that may impact the market.

In conclusion, property and market analysis tools provide wholesalers with valuable information that enables them to make informed investment decisions. Comparative Market Analysis, property inspection reports, market analysis platforms such as MLS, and NOI are useful tools that can help wholesalers assess the value of properties, analyze market trends, and evaluate investment opportunities. Wholesalers can also use online platforms such as Zillow, Redfin, and Trulia to obtain real-time updates. However, it is essential to interpret and analyze the data gathered effectively, taking into account the local market conditions, valuation methodologies, and external factors that may influence the investment decision. Utilizing these property and market analysis tools effectively can help wholesalers identify profitable investment opportunities and maximize returns in real estate wholesaling.

Digital Marketing Tools and Communication Tools for Team Collaboration and Client Interaction

In the fast-paced world of real estate wholesaling, effective marketing and communication are key to success. Wholesalers need to leverage digital marketing tools to reach their target audience, nurture leads, and build brand awareness. In addition, efficient communication tools facilitate team collaboration and enable seamless interaction with clients. This chapter explores the digital marketing tools available for email marketing and social media management, as well as communication tools for team collaboration and client interaction.

Digital marketing tools play a vital role in promoting business and engaging with potential clients. Email marketing platforms provide wholesalers with the ability to create and manage email campaigns, automate workflows, and track performance metrics. These tools allow wholesalers to build targeted email lists, create visually appealing email templates, and schedule automated follow-ups to nurture leads effectively. By analyzing email open rates, click-through rates, and conversion rates, wholesalers can optimize their campaigns and tailor their messaging to maximize engagement and generate valuable leads.

Social media management tools are also crucial for wholesalers to establish a strong online presence and connect with their target audience. These platforms enable wholesalers to schedule and publish social media content across various channels, monitor engagement and metrics, and engage with followers. With features such as content calendars, analytics, and social listening, wholesalers can effectively manage their social media presence, track the performance of their posts, and engage with their audience in a timely and personalized manner.

When it comes to communication within the wholesaling team and interacting with clients, the right tools can greatly enhance efficiency and collaboration. Collaboration and project management platforms, such as Trello, Asana, or Basecamp, enable teams to organize tasks, set deadlines, and track progress in a centralized and visually appealing manner. These tools facilitate efficient communication and task delegation, ensuring that everyone is on the same page and workflow is streamlined.

In addition to project management tools, video conferencing platforms, such as Zoom or Microsoft Teams, have become essential for remote team collaboration. These tools allow wholesalers to conduct virtual meetings, share screens, and collaborate in real-time, regardless of geographical locations. Video conferencing platforms enable face-to-face interactions, fostering stronger communication and team cohesion.

To facilitate client interaction, customer relationship management (CRM) platforms, as discussed earlier in the previous interaction on CRM systems, are indispensable. CRM platforms provide wholesalers with a centralized database of client information, including contact details, communication history, and deal progress. This allows wholesalers to effectively communicate with clients, track interactions, and provide personalized experiences. CRM platforms often integrate features such as email templates, task reminders, and document sharing, further streamlining client communication and enhancing customer relationships.

In conclusion, digital marketing tools, such as email marketing platforms and social media management tools, are essential for wholesalers to effectively promote their business and engage with their target audience. These tools enable wholesalers to create and manage email campaigns, nurture leads, and build a strong online presence through social media channels. Additionally, communication tools, including collaboration platforms and video conferencing tools, enhance team collaboration and communication, regardless of physical location. CRM platforms facilitate seamless client interaction, ensuring efficient communication, personalized experiences, and strong customer relationships. By leveraging the power of these marketing and communication platforms, wholesalers can enhance their marketing strategies, streamline team collaboration, and provide exceptional client experiences in the competitive world of real estate wholesaling.

The Importance of Digital Document Management for Contracts and Paperwork, and Recommended E-Signature Platforms to Facilitate Faster Transactions

Effective document management plays a critical role in streamlining real estate wholesaling transactions. The use of digital document management systems is becoming increasingly popular, and for a good reason. In addition, digital document signing tools have facilitated the need for physical paperwork, making it easier for wholesalers to facilitate fast transactions. This chapter explores the importance of digital document management and the recommended e-signature platforms used to facilitate faster transactions.

Real estate deals require a lot of paperwork, including offer letters, contracts, closing documents, and various legal forms. Digital document management systems enable wholesalers to store, manage, and retrieve these documents in a centralized and secure online platform, allowing for easy access and transfer of information. These systems promote efficient collaboration by providing authorized users access to specific documents, features such as version history tracking to ensure only the current versions of documents are being used, and ensure security compliance.

One of the key benefits of adopting digital document management systems for contract management and paperwork is the ability to store documents in a more organized and secure manner. These systems allow wholesalers to organize their documents by transaction, client, or type, ensuring critical documents are not lost or misplaced. Additionally, document management systems provide secure access to sensitive information, assist in streamlining regulatory compliance, and tracking document revisions, among other benefits.

The use of e-signature platforms has revolutionized the way documents can be signed, dramatically reducing the need for physical paperwork. Rather than printing, signing, and scanning documents individually, e-signature platforms provide a more streamlined, collaborative, and efficient process, saving wholesalers time and money. By integrating with document management systems, e-signature platforms enable wholesalers to quickly and securely sign documents from any device, anywhere in the world, enhancing efficiency and maximizing productivity.

Several e-signature platforms, including DocuSign, HelloSign, SignNow, and Adobe Sign, are used within the real estate industry due to their easy-to-use and secure features. These platforms offer a range of features that enable wholesalers to customize workflows and processes, track document status, and provide recipients with a fully digital signing experience. The use of e-signature tools also helps wholesalers maintain compliance with legal and regulatory requirements, such as the Electronic Signatures in Global and National Commerce (ESIGN) Act and the Uniform Electronic Transactions Act (UETA).

In conclusion, digital document management and e-signature platforms have transformed the way real estate wholesalers conduct transactions. Document management systems provide a centralized and secure platform for storing, managing, and collaborating on critical documents. E-signature platforms facilitate faster transactions by allowing wholesalers to sign and share documents electronically, reducing the need for printing, scanning, and mailing documents. DocuSign, HelloSign, SignNow, and Adobe Sign are some of the recommended e-signature tools used within the industry. By adopting digital document management and e-signature tools, wholesalers can streamline their transaction processes, reduce paperwork, and improve overall productivity.

Digital Marketing Tools and Communication Tools for Team Collaboration and Client Interaction

In the fast-paced world of real estate wholesaling, effective marketing and communication are key to success. Wholesalers need to leverage digital marketing tools to reach their target audience, nurture leads, and build brand awareness. In addition, efficient communication tools facilitate team collaboration and enable seamless interaction with clients. This chapter explores the digital marketing tools available for email marketing and social media management, as well as communication tools for team collaboration and client interaction.

Digital marketing tools play a vital role in promoting business and engaging with potential clients. Email marketing platforms provide wholesalers with the ability to create and manage email campaigns, automate workflows, and track performance metrics. These tools allow wholesalers to build targeted email lists, create visually appealing email templates, and schedule automated follow-ups to nurture leads effectively. By analyzing email open rates, click-through rates, and conversion rates, wholesalers can optimize their campaigns and tailor their messaging to maximize engagement and generate valuable leads.

Social media management tools are also crucial for wholesalers to establish a strong online presence and connect with their target audience. These platforms enable wholesalers to schedule and publish social media content across various channels, monitor engagement and metrics, and engage with followers. With features such as content calendars, analytics, and social listening, wholesalers can effectively manage their social media presence, track the performance of their posts, and engage with their audience in a timely and personalized manner.

When it comes to communication within the wholesaling team and interacting with clients, the right tools can greatly enhance efficiency and collaboration. Collaboration and project management platforms, such as Trello, Asana, or Basecamp, enable teams to organize tasks, set deadlines, and track progress in a centralized and visually appealing manner. These tools facilitate efficient communication and task delegation, ensuring that everyone is on the same page and workflow is streamlined.

In addition to project management tools, video conferencing platforms, such as Zoom or Microsoft Teams, have become essential for remote team collaboration. These tools allow wholesalers to conduct virtual meetings, share screens, and collaborate in real-time, regardless of geographical locations. Video conferencing platforms enable face-to-face interactions, fostering stronger communication and team cohesion.

To facilitate client interaction, customer relationship management (CRM) platforms, as discussed earlier in the previous interaction on CRM systems, are indispensable. CRM platforms provide wholesalers with a centralized database of client information, including contact details, communication history, and deal progress. This allows wholesalers to effectively communicate with clients, track interactions, and provide personalized experiences. CRM platforms often integrate features such as email templates, task reminders, and document sharing, further streamlining client communication and enhancing customer relationships.

In conclusion, digital marketing tools, such as email marketing platforms and social media management tools, are essential for wholesalers to effectively promote their business and engage with their target audience. These tools enable wholesalers to create and manage email campaigns, nurture leads, and build a strong online presence through social media channels. Additionally, communication tools, including collaboration platforms and video conferencing tools, enhance team collaboration and communication, regardless of physical location. CRM platforms facilitate seamless client interaction, ensuring efficient communication, personalized experiences, and strong customer relationships. By leveraging the power of these marketing and communication platforms, wholesalers can enhance their marketing strategies, streamline team collaboration, and provide exceptional client experiences in the competitive world of real estate wholesaling.

Software for Automating Repetitive Tasks (e.g., Scheduling, Data Entry), and Productivity Tools to Help Manage Tasks and Deadlines Effectively

Real estate wholesalers juggle multiple tasks simultaneously, from sourcing properties and negotiating deals to coordinating with buyers and sellers. Automating repetitive tasks can save wholesalers time and increase productivity, allowing for more focus on high-value activities. Productivity tools can help manage tasks and deadlines efficiently, reducing stress and ensuring that nothing falls through the cracks. This chapter explores software for automating repetitive tasks and productivity tools for effective task and deadline management.

Automating repetitive tasks can lead to significant time savings. Tools such as Zapier, IFTTT (If This Then That), and Microsoft Power Automate enable wholesalers to automate task workflows, reducing the manual and repetitive effort. These software tools connect with various applications and automate tasks such as scheduling appointments, sending emails, and data entry. When integrated with other tools used by wholesalers, these automations can significantly reduce time spent on mundane tasks, leading to increased productivity and efficiency.

Another critical productivity tool for task management is task management software. Tools like Trello, Asana, and Monday.com allow for the creation of to-do lists, assigning tasks to team members, and tracking progress. These tools enable wholesalers to organize their work and ensure that nothing falls through the cracks. They can set deadlines for tasks, track time spent on tasks, and assign priorities to ensure that critical tasks are completed on time.

Additionally, calendar and scheduling software can help wholesalers manage their time effectively. These tools allow for the scheduling of meetings, appointments, and other events, and can be integrated with email clients like Microsoft Outlook and Google Calendar. Wholesalers can use these tools to set reminders, block out off-hours and avoid scheduling conflicts. By streamlining their scheduling, wholesalers can optimize their day-to-day activities and ensure they stay on top of appointments, meetings and deadlines.

Another productivity tool for effective time management is time-tracking software. Toggl, RescueTime, and Clockify are examples of tools that automatically record time spent on various tasks. By tracking their time accurately, wholesalers can identify areas where they can optimize time spent and make better-informed decisions about work priorities. Moreover, they can track billable hours accurately and improve invoicing to enhance revenue generation.

In conclusion, automation and productivity tools are instrumental in increasing efficiency, saving time, and reducing stress. Automating repetitive tasks through tools such as Zapier, IFTTT, and Microsoft Power Automate can significantly improve efficiency. Task management software, calendar and scheduling software, as well as time-tracking software, can help manage tasks and deadlines effectively, leading to optimized day-to-day activity and better work outcomes. By leveraging these tools to streamline tasks and increase productivity, wholesalers can focus on high-value activities, leading to success in the real estate industry.

Importance of Securing Sensitive Business and Client Data, and Recommended Practices and Tools for Data Encryption and Backup

In the real estate industry, dealing with sensitive business and client data is paramount. Protecting this data from unauthorized access, loss, or damage is crucial to maintain trust and confidentiality. Data security ensures that sensitive information remains safe and protected, while data backup allows for quick recovery in the event of data loss or system failure. This chapter explores the importance of securing sensitive business and client data and recommends best practices and tools for data encryption and backup.

The importance of data security cannot be overstated. Wholesalers handle a vast amount of confidential information, including financial records, customer data, contracts, and property details. Breaches in data security can have severe consequences, including financial loss, reputational damage, and legal liabilities. It is essential for wholesalers to adopt robust security measures to protect sensitive data from unauthorized access, theft, or loss.

One of the recommended best practices for data security is data encryption. Encryption involves converting data into a format that can only be accessed or decrypted with a specific encryption key. By encrypting sensitive data, wholesalers can ensure that even if it is intercepted, it remains unreadable and unusable to unauthorized individuals. Tools like BitLocker, VeraCrypt, or FileVault offer encryption capabilities for files, folders, or entire disk drives, providing an extra layer of protection.

Implementing strong access controls is another critical aspect of data security. Wholesalers should employ measures such as strong passwords, multi-factor authentication, and role-based access control (RBAC) to restrict access to sensitive data. Regularly reviewing and updating access privileges and permissions helps ensure that only authorized individuals have access to specific data, reducing the risk of unauthorized data exposure.

Regular data backups are essential for data protection and quick recovery in the event of data loss or system failure. Wholesalers should have a proper data backup strategy that includes both local and offsite backups. Local backups, such as using external hard drives or network-attached storage (NAS), provide quick access to data for everyday recovery needs. Offsite backups, such as cloud-based backup solutions like Backblaze, Carbonite, or CrashPlan, offer an additional layer of protection in case of physical damage or theft.

Wholesalers should also consider implementing intrusion detection and prevention systems (IDPS). These systems monitor network traffic, identify suspicious activities, and take proactive measures to prevent unauthorized access or attacks. IDPS solutions like Snort, Suricata, or Cisco Firepower provide real-time monitoring, alerting, and incident response capabilities to safeguard data and network infrastructure.

Furthermore, ongoing employee training and awareness programs are crucial for maintaining data security. Wholesalers should educate their staff about data security best practices, such as recognizing phishing attempts, safeguarding login credentials, and reporting suspicious activities. By fostering a culture of security awareness, wholesalers can minimize the risk of human error and improve overall data security posture.

In conclusion, securing sensitive business and client data is of utmost importance in the real estate industry. By implementing recommended practices such as data encryption, strong access controls, regular data backups, intrusion detection and prevention systems, and employee training programs, wholesalers can enhance data security and protect against unauthorized access or data loss. These proactive measures ensure the integrity, confidentiality, and availability of data, building trust with clients and mitigating potential risks.

Conclusion:

In this chapter, we have explored two critical aspects of running a successful real estate wholesaling business: automation and productivity tools, and data security and backup solutions. These tools and technologies play a significant role in enhancing efficiency, protecting sensitive data, and ensuring smooth operations. Let's recap the essential tools and technologies discussed:

1. Automation and Productivity Tools: We discussed software for automating repetitive tasks and improving productivity. Tools like Zapier, IFTTT, and Microsoft Power Automate enable wholesalers to automate workflows, saving time and increasing efficiency. Task management software such as Trello, Asana, and Monday.com help in organizing and tracking tasks and deadlines effectively. Calendar and scheduling software streamline appointment management, while time-tracking software provides insights into time utilization and enhances revenue generation.

2. Data Security and Backup Solutions: We highlighted the importance of securing sensitive business and client data and provided recommended practices and tools for data encryption and backup. Employing data encryption tools like BitLocker, VeraCrypt, or FileVault protects data from unauthorized access. Implementing access controls, regular data backups (local and offsite), and intrusion detection and prevention systems (IDPS) safeguards against data loss, system failure, and unauthorized access. Ongoing employee training and awareness programs ensure a culture of security and minimize risks associated with human error.

To stay competitive and efficient in the real estate wholesaling industry, it is crucial for businesses to adopt these technologies. By embracing automation and productivity tools, wholesalers can streamline their operations, save time, and focus on high-value activities. Additionally, implementing robust data security measures and backup solutions protects sensitive information, builds trust with clients, and mitigates potential risks.

It is important to recognize that the real estate industry is constantly evolving, and technology plays a vital role in staying ahead of the competition. By embracing these tools and technologies, wholesalers can position themselves as efficient, reliable, and trustworthy partners for their clients. Moreover, adopting these technologies demonstrates a commitment to professionalism and client data protection.

In conclusion, the integration of automation and productivity tools, as well as data security and backup solutions, is essential for the success of a real estate wholesaling business. By harnessing the power of these technologies, wholesalers can streamline their operations, protect sensitive information, and elevate their competitiveness in the market. Embrace these tools and technologies to stay at the forefront of the industry and drive efficiency and success.

Part III: Financial Management

Financial management is a crucial aspect of any business, including real estate wholesaling. It involves planning, organizing, directing, and controlling financial resources to maximize profitability, minimize costs, and achieve long-term financial stability. Effective financial management empowers wholesalers to make informed decisions, allocate resources efficiently, and navigate the dynamic landscape of the real estate market.

In the realm of real estate wholesaling, financial management encompasses various key areas. These include budgeting, cash flow management, financial analysis, risk assessment, and strategic financial planning. A comprehensive understanding of these components allows wholesalers to optimize their financial performance and mitigate potential risks.

Budgeting plays a fundamental role in financial management by providing a blueprint for allocating financial resources effectively. Creating a well-structured budget helps wholesalers track income, expenses, and investments. It facilitates decision-making, prioritizes expenditures, and ensures that financial goals align with business objectives. By maintaining a well-planned budget, wholesalers can anticipate financial needs, identify areas for cost optimization, and confidently plan for future growth.

Cash flow management is another critical aspect of financial management for real estate wholesalers. Effectively managing cash flow ensures that there are sufficient funds available to cover operational expenses, investments, and unexpected contingencies. Wholesalers must monitor incoming and outgoing cash flows, optimize receivable and payable cycles, and maintain a healthy liquidity position. Utilizing tools like cash flow projections, invoice tracking systems, and financial software can help to streamline cash flow management and ensure financial stability.
Financial analysis provides wholesalers with valuable insights into the performance and profitability of their business. By analyzing financial statements, ratios, and key performance indicators (KPIs), wholesalers can evaluate the financial health of their operations. This analysis aids in identifying areas of strength and weakness, making informed decisions, and addressing potential challenges proactively. Additionally, it enables wholesalers to assess the viability of potential deals, evaluate return on investment (ROI), and identify opportunities for growth and expansion.

Risk assessment is an integral part of financial management in real estate wholesaling. Wholesalers must identify, assess, and manage various financial risks such as market volatility, credit risks, and liquidity risks. By conducting thorough risk assessments, wholesalers can develop risk mitigation strategies, diversify their investment portfolio, and ensure that their financial resources are protected. Implementing risk management practices, such as hedging strategies, insurance coverage, and contingency planning, minimizes the impact of unforeseen events and enhances financial resilience.

Strategic financial planning is a forward-looking component of financial management that involves setting long-term financial goals and developing strategies to achieve them. Wholesalers must consider factors such as market trends, competition, regulatory changes, and capital requirements when formulating their financial plans. Strategic financial planning enables wholesalers to align financial objectives with overall business objectives, identify investment opportunities, and make informed decisions about financing options, expansion plans, and business partnerships.

In conclusion, financial management is an essential discipline for real estate wholesalers. By mastering the art of financial management, wholesalers can optimize their financial performance, minimize risks, and capitalize on growth opportunities. Understanding the intricacies of budgeting, cash flow management, financial analysis, risk assessment, and strategic financial planning empowers wholesalers to make sound financial decisions and navigate the ever-changing landscape of the real estate market.

Chapter 5: Exploring Financing Options

In the dynamic world of real estate wholesaling, understanding financing options is of paramount importance for success. Proper financing can provide the necessary capital to acquire and assign properties effectively, while a lack of knowledge in this area can hinder opportunities and limit growth. This comprehensive guide will delve into the significance of understanding financing options in real estate wholesaling and shed light on how proper financing can impact the success of wholesaling ventures.

Importance of Understanding Financing Options:

1. Access to Capital: Financing options open doors to the capital needed for acquiring properties in real estate wholesaling. Whether it be purchasing properties for inventory or securing earnest money deposits, having a solid understanding of financing options ensures that wholesalers can seize opportunities that arise in the market.

2. Flexibility in Deal Structuring: A detailed knowledge of financing alternatives allows wholesalers to navigate different deal structures and optimize their potential for profitability. Understanding how financing works empowers wholesalers to negotiate favorable terms, obtain higher offers, and structure deals that align with their business objectives.

3. Competitive Advantage: In the highly competitive real estate market, having a thorough understanding of financing options can give wholesalers a significant edge. By leveraging knowledge of creative financing techniques, wholesalers can craft unique solutions that other market participants may overlook. This advantage can help wholesalers secure better deals, attract quality investors, and establish a reputation as a trusted and knowledgeable professional.

Overview of How Proper Financing Impacts Wholesaling Ventures:

1. Property Acquisition: Proper financing is the lifeline of real estate wholesaling. The ability to secure funding sources allows wholesalers

to acquire properties with ease. Whether through traditional mortgage loans, hard money lenders, or private investors, having access to capital ensures wholesalers can swiftly close deals and efficiently move properties through the wholesaling process.

2. Increased Deal Flow: Understanding financing options expands the possibility of engaging in more significant deals. Wholesalers who have the financial capacity to handle larger transactions can tap into a wider range of opportunities and diversify their portfolios. This flexibility allows wholesalers to take advantage of fluctuating market conditions and capitalize on lucrative deals that may not be accessible to those with limited financing knowledge.

3. Mitigating Risk:Proper financing helps wholesalers mitigate risks associated with real estate wholesaling. By having a solid understanding of loan terms, interest rates, and repayment schedules, wholesalers can make informed decisions when selecting financing options. Additionally, diverse financing options can act as a buffer against market fluctuations, enabling wholesalers to adapt and navigate through challenging economic conditions.

4. Scaling and Growth: As wholesalers gain expertise and expand their operations, proper financing becomes vital for scaling and sustaining growth. Access to timely capital ensures wholesalers can meet increasing demand, fund marketing campaigns, and embark on new ventures. The ability to leverage financing options strategically bolsters business expansion, opens new market opportunities, and potentially leads to long-term success.

In the realm of real estate wholesaling, understanding financing options is a fundamental aspect that cannot be overlooked. It is the cornerstone of acquiring properties, negotiating deals, and scaling a wholesaling business. Aspiring wholesalers who possess comprehensive knowledge of financing alternatives gain a competitive advantage in the market and increase their potential for success. By recognizing the significance of understanding financing options and its impact on wholesaling ventures, individuals can navigate the dynamic real estate landscape with confidence and achieve their goals in this rewarding industry.

Personal Savings and Self-Financing

Personal Savings and Self-Financing refers to the practice of utilizing one's own personal funds to finance the establishment and ongoing operations of a business venture. This approach allows entrepreneurs to rely on their own financial resources rather than seeking external sources of funding, such as loans or investments.

The risks associated with Personal Savings and Self-Financing are twofold. Firstly, by utilizing personal savings, individuals put their own financial security at stake. If the business fails, personal funds may be depleted, leading to significant financial repercussions. Secondly, relying solely on personal funds may limit the growth potential of the business. Without access to additional capital, it can be challenging to expand operations or pursue new opportunities.

Despite these risks, there are several benefits associated with Personal Savings and Self-Financing. Firstly, it offers a high degree of independence and control over the business. Entrepreneurs can make decisions without external influences and retain full ownership of their venture. Additionally, self-financing eliminates the need to pay interest on loans or share profits with investors, resulting in a higher degree of financial autonomy.

Moreover, Personal Savings and Self-Financing provides a sense of confidence and commitment to the business. By investing their own money, entrepreneurs demonstrate their belief in the venture's potential, which can be appealing to prospective partners, lenders, or investors. It also allows for greater flexibility in decision-making and reallocating funds as per the business's evolving needs.

In summary, Personal Savings and Self-Financing entail using personal funds for business purposes, offering advantages such as independence, control, and a strong commitment to the venture. However, it is crucial to consider the potential risks involved, including personal financial exposure and limited growth opportunities. Entrepreneurs should weigh these factors carefully before deciding on the most suitable financing approach for their business.

Traditional Bank Loans are one of the most common forms of financing for businesses, including those in the real estate industry. There are several types of bank loans available for real estate businesses, including commercial mortgages, construction loans, and bridge loans.

Commercial mortgages are long-term loans intended for properties used for business purposes, such as office buildings, retail spaces, or warehouses. These loans have fixed or adjustable interest rates and can span 10 to 30 years. Construction loans, on the other hand, are short-term loans used to finance the construction of new buildings or major renovations. Finally, Bridge loans are a type of short-term financing that enables real estate investors to acquire new properties before selling existing ones.

The requirements for securing Traditional Bank Loans depend on the type of loan and the lender's criteria. Generally, real estate businesses need to provide a detailed business plan and financial statements outlining their ability to repay the loan. Collateral may also be required to secure the loan, such as the property being financed or other business assets.

The benefits of Traditional Bank Loans include lower interest rates, longer repayment terms, and potentially higher loan amounts compared to other financing options. Additionally, securing a bank loan can establish business credit and help build a stronger relationship with the lender.

However, there are also several drawbacks to consider. Traditional Bank Loans can involve a lengthy and complex application process, and approval is not guaranteed. Repayment terms can also be inflexible, and there may be penalties for early repayment. Additionally, securing a loan may require providing collateral and personal guarantees, which could put personal assets at risk.

In conclusion, Traditional Bank Loans can provide significant benefits for real estate businesses, including lower interest rates, longer repayment terms, and higher loan amounts. However, the requirements for securing a loan can be demanding, and there are also potential drawbacks, such as inflexible repayment terms and personal financial exposure. It is important to carefully consider the pros and cons of Traditional Bank Loans and evaluate alternative financing options before deciding on the most appropriate approach for your business.

Private Lenders play a significant role in real estate wholesaling by providing loans to investors for property purchases and renovations. Unlike traditional banks, private lenders are individuals or groups that specialize in providing short-term financing solutions for real estate investment projects.

Finding and approaching private lenders can be done through networking or referrals, local real estate investment clubs, or online platforms. It is crucial to approach private lenders with a solid business plan and a clear understanding of the specific property and investment opportunity. Creating a professional presentation and demonstrating a track record of successful deals can also help attract potential lenders.

The terms and conditions of private lending vary depending on the lender. Private lenders typically charge higher interest rates compared to traditional banks and may require a higher down payment or shorter repayment period, such as six to 24 months. Additionally, private lending may require that property inspections and appraisals be conducted to determine the property's value and verify renovation costs.

Despite higher costs, private lending has several benefits, such as flexibility, faster lending decisions, and access to funds for deals that traditional banks may not approve. The ability to negotiate terms and conditions with a private lender allows for a more customized financing solution tailored to the specific needs of the borrower. Private lending can also provide an opportunity to establish a long-term lending partnership between the lender and investor.

In summary, private lending is a useful financing option for real estate investors seeking flexible and customized financing solutions for their projects. Finding and approaching private lenders can be accomplished through networking or referral channels, and terms and conditions vary depending on the lender. While private lending may involve higher costs, it also provides several benefits, such as faster lending decisions and access to funds for deals that traditional banks may not approve.

Hard Money Loans are a type of short-term financing provided by private individuals or companies, commonly known as "hard money lenders," who focus on real estate investment opportunities. These loans are asset-based, meaning they are secured by the property itself rather than the borrower's creditworthiness.

Hard money loans typically have a faster approval process compared to traditional loans, making them suitable for time-sensitive real estate investments or when traditional financing is not readily available. These loans are primarily used for fix-and-flip projects, rehabilitation, or purchasing properties in poor condition that would not qualify for traditional financing.

One of the main advantages of hard money loans is their accessibility. Hard money lenders are primarily concerned with the value of the property being used as collateral and the borrower's exit strategy rather than their credit history or income. This allows real estate investors with less-than-ideal credit or limited income documentation to secure financing for their projects.

Another advantage is the speed at which hard money loans can be obtained. Compared to traditional loans, hard money lenders can provide funding within days or weeks, allowing investors to quickly take advantage of time-sensitive opportunities.

However, hard money loans come with certain disadvantages. The interest rates on hard money loans are typically higher than those of traditional loans, ranging from 8% to 15% or even higher. Additionally, hard money loans often have shorter terms, typically ranging from six months to two years, which can put pressure on borrowers to complete their projects swiftly and sell or refinance the property.

In summary, hard money loans are short-term, asset-based financing options primarily used for real estate investments. They are most appropriate for fix-and-flip projects, rehabilitation, or when traditional financing is not available. The advantages of hard money loans include accessibility regardless of credit history and quick approval and funding. However, the drawbacks include higher interest rates and shorter repayment terms. It is essential to carefully evaluate the specific circumstances and financial needs before deciding whether a hard money loan is the right choice for a real estate investment.

Real Estate Partnerships are a common strategy used by investors to pool resources and capitalize on funding opportunities. By forming partnerships, real estate investors can access additional capital, share responsibilities, and leverage each other's expertise and networks.

When structuring partnership agreements, it is crucial to clearly define the roles and responsibilities of each partner, as well as the terms of the partnership. Some important aspects to consider include:

1. Contribution: Partners should determine how much capital each party will contribute to the partnership and whether contributions will be in the form of cash, property, or other assets. It is also important to establish how profits and losses will be distributed among partners.

2. Decision-making: Partnership agreements should outline the decision-making process, including how major decisions, such as property acquisitions or sales, will be made. Consider whether decisions will be made collectively or if one partner will have decision-making authority.

3. Exit Strategy: It is crucial to establish how and when the partnership will be dissolved or how partners can exit the partnership if necessary. This may include provisions for selling the property, buying out a partner's share, or other exit mechanisms.

Additionally, managing relationships with financial partners involves open communication, trust, and transparency. Here are some tips for effective relationship management:

1. Regular Communication: Maintain open lines of communication with your financial partners. Provide them with regular updates on the progress of the investment, financial performance, and any potential challenges or opportunities.

2. Transparency: Be transparent about the financials and performance of the partnership. Provide detailed financial reports and ensure that all partners have access to necessary information.

3. Trust and Respect: Build trust and maintain respectful relationships with your financial partners. Nurture a collaborative environment where all parties feel their input is valued and appreciated.

4. Clear Expectations: Set clear expectations from the beginning regarding roles, responsibilities, and expectations. Clearly outline how profits and losses will be shared and any milestones or goals the partnership aims to achieve.

5. Conflict Resolution: In the event of conflicts or disagreements, address them promptly and strive for a resolution that is fair and beneficial for all parties involved. Consider involving a neutral third party or mediator if necessary.

Remember, each partnership is unique, so it is recommended to consult with legal and financial professionals to ensure that the partnership agreement is tailored to your specific needs and complies with local regulations.

Government programs and grants can provide valuable financial assistance for real estate investments. Here are some key points to consider regarding available options, qualification criteria, and application processes:

1. Government-Backed Loans: Government-backed loans are provided by government agencies or institutions and typically offer favorable terms and lower interest rates. Examples include the Federal Housing Administration (FHA) loans and Veterans Affairs (VA) loans in the United States. To qualify for these loans, specific criteria must be met, such as creditworthiness, income requirements, and property eligibility. The application process typically involves completing an application, providing necessary documentation, and working with an approved lender.

2. Housing Assistance Programs: These programs are designed to assist low-income individuals or families in obtaining affordable housing. Examples include the Section 8 Housing Choice Voucher program in the United States, which provides rental subsidies to eligible individuals. Qualification criteria vary depending on the specific program and may consider factors such as income, family size, and housing needs. To apply, individuals typically need to complete an application, submit required documentation, and meet with program representatives for evaluation.

3. Tax Incentives and Grants: Governments may offer tax incentives or grants to promote real estate development, revitalization, or energy-efficient improvements. These incentives can include tax credits, exemptions, or grants for eligible projects. Qualification criteria vary based on the specific incentive or grant, and applications typically involve submitting detailed project proposals, financial information, and compliance with program guidelines. It is essential to research available programs and consult with tax professionals or government entities for detailed information and guidance.

4. Research and Application Process: To identify relevant government programs and grants, conduct thorough research at the local, regional, or national level, depending on your location. Government websites, housing authorities, and economic development agencies are valuable sources of information. Determine the eligibility criteria, review application requirements, and understand the deadlines and submission procedures. It is crucial to submit complete and accurate applications within the specified timelines to maximize the chances of approval.

Remember, specific government programs and grants for real estate can vary by country, state, or municipality. It is important to stay updated on the latest information, as programs may change, new options may become available, or existing programs may be phased out. Consulting with professionals knowledgeable in real estate and government programs can provide valuable insights and guidance throughout the qualification and application processes.

Crowdfunding and syndication are two popular methods for raising funds for real estate investments. Here's an overview of how you can leverage these approaches:

1. Crowdfunding Platforms: Crowdfunding platforms serve as online marketplaces connecting real estate developers or sponsors with potential investors. These platforms allow individuals to invest smaller amounts of money, pooling their resources to fund larger real estate projects. To leverage crowdfunding platforms for real estate investments, follow these steps:

   a. Research Platforms: Explore different crowdfunding platforms specializing in real estate. Consider factors such as platform reputation, track record, fees, investment opportunities, and investor protections.

   b. Due Diligence: Review investment opportunities available on the platform. The sponsor will typically provide details about the project, including financial projections, risk assessments, property information, and planned returns. Conduct thorough due diligence by analyzing the provided information and assessing the reputation and experience of the sponsor.

   c. Investment Process: Once you've selected a project, follow the platform's investment process. This usually involves creating an account, completing required documentation (such as investor accreditation forms), and transferring funds. Be mindful of minimum investment requirements and any associated fees.

   d. Monitor Investment: After making an investment, stay updated on the project's progress and performance through regular reports and updates provided by the sponsor. Monitor financial and operational aspects of the investment to ensure alignment with your goals and expectations.

2. Real Estate Syndication: Real estate syndication involves pooling financial resources from multiple investors to collectively invest in a real estate project. Here are the basics of real estate syndication:

   a. Syndication Structure: A syndication typically involves a General Partner (GP), who manages the project and has expertise in real estate, and Limited Partners (LPs), who contribute capital but have a passive role. The GP is responsible for the day-to-day operations of the investment.

   b. Partner Roles and Agreements: Syndication agreements outline the roles, responsibilities, and profit-sharing arrangements among partners. The agreement specifies the GP's compensation, how profits and losses are distributed, and the terms for potential exits or sale of the property.

   c. Participation Process: To participate in real estate syndication, research syndicators or real estate companies that offer investment opportunities. Evaluate their track record, expertise, and the types of projects they undertake. Once you find a syndicator, review their offering documents, such as private placement memorandums or subscription agreements, and consult legal and financial professionals to ensure understanding and compliance.

   d. Investment and Partnership: If you decide to proceed, invest the required capital as stipulated in the offering documents. You become a limited partner, typically with voting rights related to important decisions. Once the project is underway, monitor progress, attend partner meetings, and stay informed about the investment's performance.

Remember, both crowdfunding and syndication involve investment risks, and it's crucial to conduct thorough research, evaluate opportunities, and consult professionals as needed to make informed investment decisions.

Creative financing strategies can be useful for real estate investors looking to acquire or sell properties. Here is an overview of some popular techniques and their uses:

1. Seller Financing: Seller financing involves the seller lending money to the buyer to purchase the property, instead of the buyer obtaining the funds from a traditional lender. Common terms for these loans include interest rates, repayment periods, and collateral agreements. The benefits of using seller financing can include more flexible terms, faster processing, and avoiding lender fees. Seller financing can be used in many real estate transactions, including commercial and residential properties.

2. Lease Options: Lease options involve the buyer leasing a property for a defined period with an option to buy it at a predetermined price at the end of the period. The buyer often pays an upfront fee for the right to purchase the property and may also pay an additional premium for the option to buy. Lease options can provide benefits for both buyers and sellers, such as enabling buyers to get into properties with less money upfront and allowing sellers more time to find buyers.

3. Subject-To Financing: Subject-to financing involves the buyer taking over the seller's existing mortgage, with the balance owed to the lender remaining the same. This type of financing can be beneficial to the buyer, as it may allow them to acquire the property without obtaining a new loan. However, subject-to financing can be risky, as the buyer must ensure they can manage the mortgage payments and maintain the property's value.

4. Legal Considerations: It's important to understand the legal implications of using creative financing strategies in real estate transactions. Each strategy may have unique legal requirements, including disclosures, documentation, and compliance with relevant

laws. Consulting with experienced legal professionals can help mitigate risks and ensure compliance with applicable regulations.

5. Practical Applications: Each creative financing strategy has practical applications depending on the investor's goals and preferences. For example, seller financing can be beneficial for sellers looking to sell their property quickly, while lease options may be more advantageous for buyers looking to acquire properties with limited finances upfront. Careful evaluation of the specific situation and long-term objectives can help investors determine the best financing strategy to pursue.

In summary, creative financing strategies can provide opportunities for investors to buy or sell properties with more flexibility and unique terms. Consider the legal implications of each strategy, establish clear objectives, and seek expert guidance where necessary.

In conclusion, exploring the various financing options in real estate can be crucial for investors seeking strategic approaches to meet their financial needs. Let's summarize the key points discussed and emphasize the importance of evaluating each option's benefits and risks.

We discussed several financing options, including crowdfunding and syndication, seller financing, lease options, and subject-to financing. Each option has its unique strategic use and can be tailored to specific investment goals.

Crowdfunding and syndication offer the opportunity to participate in real estate projects through online platforms, allowing investors to pool resources and invest in larger endeavors. These options provide diversification and access to projects with lower entry barriers.

Seller financing enables buyers to acquire properties by securing loans directly from sellers, ensuring more flexibility with terms and potentially faster transactions. Lease options, on the other hand, allow buyers to lease a property with an option to buy it at a predetermined price in the future. This approach can be advantageous for those facing financial constraints or seeking more time for decision-making.

Subject-to financing allows buyers to assume the seller's existing mortgage, bypassing the need for a new loan. This strategy can be suitable for investors seeking to acquire properties without going through extensive financing processes but requires careful consideration of mortgage obligations.

To make informed decisions, it is crucial for investors to evaluate their financial needs against the benefits and risks of each financing option. Consider factors such as cash flow requirements, desired investment timeline, risk tolerance, legal considerations, and exit strategies.

Investors should also consult professionals such as attorneys, accountants, and financial advisors to ensure compliance with legal requirements and to gain a comprehensive understanding of the risks involved.

By taking the time to assess financial needs, objectives, and risk appetite, investors can select the most suitable financing option for their real estate ventures. Remember, each option has its benefits and drawbacks, and thorough evaluation is essential in determining the right fit for your investment strategy.

In conclusion, the world of real estate financing presents a range of creative options that can be tailored to meet investors' unique needs. By carefully considering the strategic uses, benefits, and risks of each option, investors can navigate the market with greater confidence and achieve their desired financial outcomes.

Chapter 6: Cash Flow and Financial Operations

Introduction to Financial Management in Real Estate Wholesaling

Financial management plays a crucial role in the success and sustainability of any business, including real estate wholesaling. This introductory chapter aims to shed light on the importance of financial management specifically within the context of real estate wholesaling, as well as simplify the concept of cash flow to make it more accessible and understandable for individuals in this industry.

One of the primary reasons why financial management is crucial in real estate wholesaling is its direct impact on profitability. Effective financial management practices help ensure that expenses are controlled, revenues are maximized, and overall profitability is optimized. By carefully managing finances, wholesalers can identify areas where cost reductions can be made, negotiate better deals with suppliers, and effectively price their properties to generate higher profits.

In addition to profitability, financial management also helps mitigate risks and uncertainties in the real estate wholesaling business. By properly analyzing financial data, wholesalers can identify potential risks, such as market fluctuations or changes in property values. This allows them to take proactive measures and develop contingency plans to navigate these challenges.

Furthermore, financial management serves as a critical tool for decision-making in real estate wholesaling. Wholesalers often face complex decisions, such as whether to invest in a particular property, expand their business operations, or secure financing for new projects. By using financial analysis techniques, wholesalers can assess the potential profitability and risks associated with these decisions, enabling them to make informed choices that align with their long-term goals.

Understanding cash flow is a fundamental aspect of financial management in any business, including real estate wholesaling. Cash flow refers to the movement of money in and out of a business over a given period. It encompasses the inflows of revenue from property sales, rental income, and other sources, as well as the outflows related to expenses, such as property acquisition costs, marketing expenses, and operating expenses.

To make the concept of cash flow more accessible and easier to comprehend, this chapter will break down its components and explain how it relates to the day-to-day operations of a real estate wholesaling business. It will highlight the importance of effective cash flow management in ensuring the smooth functioning of the business, meeting financial obligations, and maintaining liquidity.

Moreover, this chapter will aim to simplify financial concepts to help individuals in the real estate wholesaling industry better understand and apply them in their businesses. Financial terminology can often be intimidating and confusing, especially for those without a background in finance. By providing clear explanations and practical examples, this chapter will make financial concepts more relatable and practical, empowering wholesalers to apply them effectively in their financial management tasks.

In summary, this chapter serves as an introduction to financial management in the context of real estate wholesaling. It emphasizes the importance of financial management for profitability, risk mitigation, and decision-making. Additionally, it aims to simplify the concept of cash flow and make financial concepts more accessible, encouraging wholesalers to effectively manage their finances for long-term success in their businesses.

Understanding Cash Flow: Importance and Difference from Profit

Cash flow is a fundamental aspect of financial management in any business, including real estate wholesaling. It refers to the movement of money in and out of a business over a specific period, typically measured monthly, quarterly, or annually. Cash flow management is the practice of efficiently monitoring, analyzing, and optimizing these inflows and outflows to ensure the smooth functioning and financial stability of the business.

Definition and Importance of Cash Flow Management:
Cash flow management involves understanding the timing and magnitude of cash inflows and outflows to maintain adequate liquidity and meet financial obligations. It provides crucial insights into the financial health of a business and serves as a key indicator of its ability to generate and utilize cash effectively.

Effective cash flow management is vital for several reasons:

1. Liquidity and Survival: Positive cash flow ensures that a business has enough liquid assets on hand to cover its expenses, pay suppliers, meet financial obligations, and sustain its operations during both normal and challenging times. Without proper cash flow management, even profitable businesses can face cash shortages and struggle to survive.

2. Operational Efficiency: Monitoring cash flow allows businesses to identify inefficiencies, such as excessive spending or delays in receivables collection, which can be optimized to enhance overall operational efficiency. By identifying cash flow bottlenecks, businesses can implement strategies to streamline their cash flow cycle and make more informed financial decisions.

3. Planning and Decision-making: Accurate cash flow projections provide a foundation for effective business planning, budgeting, and decision-making. By understanding future cash inflows and outflows, businesses can make strategic decisions about investments, expansion, and risk management. Cash flow analysis enables businesses to assess the feasibility and financial implications of potential projects or decisions.

Difference between Cash Flow and Profit:
While cash flow and profit are related, they represent different aspects of a business's financial performance:

1. Cash Flow: Cash flow focuses on the movement of actual cash in and out of a business. It captures the timing of cash inflows and outflows and reflects the availability of liquid assets to meet obligations. A positive cash flow indicates that a business has enough cash to cover expenses, invest in growth, and handle unexpected situations. Cash flow can be positive even if a business is not generating profit, and vice versa.

2. Profit: Profit, on the other hand, is the financial gain resulting from revenues exceeding expenses over a specific period. It represents the surplus left over after deducting all costs, including direct costs, operating expenses, taxes, and interest. Profit is important for assessing the long-term viability and sustainability of a business. However, profit does not necessarily translate directly into cash, as it may include non-cash items such as depreciation or changes in accounts payable or receivable.

To summarize, cash flow management is crucial for ensuring liquidity, operational efficiency, and informed decision-making in real estate wholesaling. Cash flow represents the actual movement of cash in and out of a business, whereas profit reflects the financial gain after all expenses are deducted. Understanding the difference between cash flow and profit is essential for evaluating the financial health and performance of a business accurately.

Cash Flow Analysis: Performing and Forecasting

Performing a cash flow analysis allows businesses to monitor, evaluate, and plan their cash inflows and outflows. It provides valuable insights into a company's financial health, helps identify potential liquidity issues, and facilitates effective decision-making. Here are some steps to perform a cash flow analysis:

1. Gather Financial Information: Collect all relevant financial data, such as sales and revenue records, expense records, accounts receivable and payable information, loan payments, and any other cash-related transactions. This data forms the basis for the cash flow analysis.

2. Separate Cash Flows: Categorize cash inflows and outflows into relevant categories, such as operating activities (e.g., sales revenue, rental income), investing activities (e.g., property acquisitions, equipment purchases), and financing activities (e.g., loan repayments, equity financing).

3. Calculate Net Cash Flow: Calculate the net cash flow for each category by deducting cash outflows from cash inflows. This will provide a clear picture of the cash generated or consumed by specific business activities.

4. Assess Cash Flow Patterns: Analyze the trends and patterns in your cash flow. Identify any consistent positive or negative cash flow patterns and explore the underlying reasons. This analysis can help identify areas for improvement or potential risks.

5. Cash Flow Forecasting: Develop a cash flow forecast to estimate future cash inflows and outflows. Use historical data, market trends, sales projections, and other relevant information to make reasonable assumptions for the forecast period. This forecast will assist in planning and decision-making.

Tools and Techniques for Effective Cash Flow Forecasting:

1. Spreadsheet Programs: Utilize spreadsheet software, such as Microsoft Excel or Google Sheets, to create cash flow projection

templates. These programs allow you to input historical data, perform calculations, and easily modify assumptions for future forecasts.

2. Cash Flow Forecasting Software: Consider using specialized cash flow forecasting software. These tools automate the process, provide advanced forecasting models, and offer additional features such as scenario analysis and reporting capabilities.

3. Rolling Cash Flow Forecasts: Instead of relying only on a fixed forecast, develop rolling cash flow forecasts. This approach involves updating the forecast regularly, replacing historical data with actuals, and extending the projection period. Rolling forecasts offer real-time visibility and flexibility in adapting to changing market conditions.

4. Sensitivity Analysis: Conduct sensitivity analysis to assess the impact of potential changes in key variables on cash flow. Identify factors that can influence cash flow, such as interest rates, sales volumes, or pricing, and evaluate different scenarios to determine the potential outcomes.

5. Cash Flow Monitoring Tools: Implement cash flow monitoring tools or dashboards to track and visualize cash flow in real-time. These tools can integrate with accounting systems, provide graphical representations, and generate alerts for cash flow deviations or critical thresholds.

Remember, accurate forecasting relies on reliable data, realistic assumptions, and continuous monitoring. Regularly compare the forecasted cash flow to actual results, analyze variances, and adjust forecasting models accordingly.

By performing a thorough cash flow analysis and employing suitable tools and techniques for cash flow forecasting, businesses can proactively manage their cash flow, make informed decisions, and ensure financial stability and growth.

Improving Cash Flow: Strategies and Tips

Positive cash flow is essential for the financial sustainability and growth of any business, including real estate wholesaling. To improve cash flow, businesses can implement various strategies to increase income, reduce expenses, and optimize the timing of cash inflows and outflows. Here are some strategies and tips to improve cash flow:

1. Increase Income: Explore ways to generate additional revenue streams, such as expanding services, offering new products, or targeting new markets.

2. Reduce Expenses: Look for ways to reduce expenses without sacrificing quality or productivity. Some cost-cutting measures include renegotiating contracts, outsourcing non-core activities, reducing inventory levels, and implementing energy-efficient solutions.

3. Optimize Inventory Management: Excess inventory can tie up capital and result in cash shortages. Analyze inventory turnover and identify slow-moving or obsolete products. Implement effective inventory management techniques, such as just-in-time inventory, to reduce inventory levels and improve cash flow.

4. Negotiate Payment Terms: Consider negotiating payment terms with suppliers and customers to align with the cash flow cycle. For example, request extended payment terms from suppliers or offer discounts for early payment from customers.

5. Improve Receivables Management: Manage receivables efficiently to reduce collection times and improve cash flow. Set clear payment terms, invoice promptly, follow up on overdue payments, and consider factoring or discounted invoices.

6. Review Financing Options: Review financing options, such as lines of credit, loans, or leasing, to provide additional cash flow cushion during lean periods. However, keep in mind the costs associated with financing and only borrow what is necessary.

Tips for Managing Timing Differences between Receivables and Payables:

Timing differences between receivables and payables can create significant cash flow gaps. Here are some tips to manage timing differences effectively:

1. Analyze Cash Flow Cycles: Understand the timing and magnitude of cash inflows and outflows for different business activities and optimize cash flow cycles accordingly.

2. Implement Cash Flow Forecasting: Develop a cash flow forecast to anticipate timing gaps and prepare for them accordingly. This can assist in identifying potential financing needs and implementing cost-saving measures.

3. Prioritize Payments: Prioritize payments, such as taxes, payroll, and critical suppliers, while managing timing differences.

4. Consider Factoring: Factoring involves the sale of accounts receivables to a third party at a discounted rate. This can provide immediate cash flow and reduce the impact of timing differences.

By implementing these strategies and tips, businesses can improve their cash flow management, reduce risks, and ensure financial stability and growth.

Budgeting and Financial Planning for Real Estate Wholesaling:

Creating a budget tailored to real estate wholesaling and implementing financial planning techniques can provide crucial financial control and assist in accurate forecasting. Here are some steps to create a budget and utilize it for financial control and forecasting in real estate wholesaling:

Creating a Budget Tailored to Real Estate Wholesaling:
1. Assess Income Sources: Identify and list all potential income sources in real estate wholesaling, such as assignment fees, commission income, or joint venture profits. Estimate the expected revenue for each income source.

2. Identify Expenses: Categorize and itemize all expenses specific to real estate wholesaling. These may include marketing and advertising costs, office rent, insurance premiums, legal fees, permits, and operating expenses for technology and systems.

3. Estimate Variable Expenses: Some expenses may vary depending on the transaction volume. Estimate variable expenses like due diligence costs, closing costs, and title and escrow fees based on past transactions or industry averages.

4. Allocate Resources: Once you have identified income sources and expenses, allocate resources accordingly by assigning realistic budget amounts to each category. Consider historical data, industry benchmarks, and your business goals when setting budget amounts.

5. Consider Contingencies: Set aside a contingency fund for unforeseen expenses or emergencies. This will provide a safety net and prevent budget constraints in case unexpected costs arise.

6. Regularly Review and Adjust: Review and assess your budget periodically, such as monthly or quarterly, to track actual income and expenses. Compare the actuals against the budgeted amounts and make adjustments as necessary to ensure accuracy and relevance.

Using Budgeting for Financial Control and Forecasting:

1. Financial Control: Regularly monitor your income and expenses to maintain financial control. Track your actual performance against the budget to identify any deviations, overspending, or areas where you can improve efficiency.

2. Variance Analysis: Conduct a variance analysis by comparing actual financial results to the budgeted amounts. Analyze the reasons for any significant variances and take corrective actions if necessary. This analysis will help you identify areas that require attention or adjustments to achieve your financial goals.

3. Forecasting: Utilize your budget as a foundation for financial forecasting. By analyzing historical data and trends, you can project future income and expenses and assess the financial feasibility of potential deals or growth strategies. This will help you in making informed decisions and planning for long-term financial stability.

4. Adjusting Priorities: Identify areas where you can cut costs or utilize resources more effectively based on your budget and financial forecasts. Shift priorities, allocate resources strategically, and make informed decisions to maximize profitability and minimize risks.

5. Revisit and Revise: As your business evolves, revisit your budget and financial plans regularly. Adjust your budget to reflect changing market conditions, business goals, or revised income and expense projections. By staying adaptable and flexible, you can ensure your budget remains relevant and effective.

Budgeting and financial planning are vital tools to maintain financial control, optimize cash flow, and forecast accurately in real estate wholesaling. By tailoring your budget to your specific business needs and leveraging it for financial control and forecasting, you can make well-informed decisions, achieve your financial goals, and ensure long-term success in real estate wholesaling.

Financial Reporting for Real Estate Wholesaling:

Financial reporting is crucial for real estate wholesalers to track and analyze the financial performance of their business. Key financial reports, namely the cash flow statement, balance sheet, and income statement, provide valuable insights into the financial health of the company. Understanding and effectively utilizing these financial reports empower wholesalers to make informed business decisions. Here's an overview of essential financial reports and their significance:

1. Cash Flow Statement:
The cash flow statement tracks the cash inflows and outflows during a specific period. It provides a comprehensive picture of how cash moves in and out of the business. Key components of the cash flow statement include:
- Operating Activities: Cash generated or consumed by the company's primary operations.
- Investing Activities: Cash flows related to the purchase or sale of long-term assets.
- Financing Activities: Cash flows from borrowings, repayments, or investments from owners.

Utilizing the Cash Flow Statement:
- Analyze the cash flow patterns to assess the liquidity and cash availability.
- Identify potential cash flow issues and take necessary measures to address them.
- Evaluate the efficiency of cash management practices and optimize working capital.

2. Balance Sheet:
The balance sheet provides a snapshot of the company's financial position at a specific point in time. It presents the assets, liabilities, and equity of the business. Key components of the balance sheet include:

- Assets: Resources owned by the business, such as cash, accounts receivable, inventory, and property.
- Liabilities: Debts and obligations owed by the business, including accounts payable, loans, and accrued expenses.
- Equity: The owner's or shareholder's investment in the business.

Utilizing the Balance Sheet:
- Assess the company's financial stability and solvency.
- Analyze the liquidity position by comparing current assets to current liabilities.
- Monitor the business's overall financial health and assess the growth potential.

3. Income Statement (Profit and Loss Statement):
The income statement reports the company's revenues, expenses, and net income or loss over a specific period. It shows the profitability of the business. Key components of the income statement include:
- Revenue: Income generated from sales, services, or other business activities.
- Expenses: Costs incurred to operate the business, including salaries, rent, marketing, and utilities.
- Net Income (Loss): The difference between total revenue and total expenses.

Utilizing the Income Statement:
- Assess the profitability and performance of the business.
- Identify trends and patterns in revenue and expenses over time.
- Make informed decisions about pricing, cost management, and revenue generation strategies.

Utilizing Financial Reports to Make Informed Business Decisions:
1. Performance Assessment: Regularly review financial reports to evaluate the business's performance against benchmarks and goals. Identify areas of strength and weakness to make informed decisions for improvement.

2. Financial Planning and Forecasting: Analyze historical financial data and utilize financial reports to forecast future revenue, expenses, and cash flow. This enables wholesalers to plan and budget effectively for future growth and profitability.

3. Investment and Expansion Decisions: Financial reports provide insights into the financial health and potential risks of the business. Use these reports to assess investment opportunities, evaluate expansion plans, and make strategic decisions based on reliable financial information.

4. Communication and Compliance: Financial reports are essential for communication with stakeholders, including investors, lenders, and regulatory authorities. Ensure accurate and transparent reporting to maintain credibility and compliance with legal and regulatory requirements.

By understanding the importance of financial reports and effectively utilizing them, real estate wholesalers can gain valuable insights into their business's financial performance. These insights enable informed decision-making, strategic planning, and financial stability in the ever-changing real estate market.

Working Capital Management in Real Estate Wholesaling:

Working capital management refers to the management of current assets and liabilities, such as cash, accounts receivable, inventory, and accounts payable, to ensure efficient day-to-day operations in a business. Effective working capital management is crucial in real estate wholesaling, where cash flow is vital to achieving success. Here are some insights into the importance of working capital management and techniques for efficient working capital management in real estate wholesaling:

Importance of Working Capital in Day-to-Day Operations:
The importance of working capital in day-to-day operations of real estate wholesaling is as follows:
1. Meeting short-term financial obligations: Working capital helps wholesalers finance short-term obligations such as paying vendors, service providers, and employees.
2. Cash Flow Management: Proper management of working capital ensures businesses have sufficient cash to meet day-to-day expenses, thus avoiding short-term cash crunches.
3. Managing the Risk of Inventory Obsolescence: Efficient management of working capital ensures that inventory is efficiently managed to reduce potential losses due to obsolescence.
4. Taking Advantage of Opportunities: Having adequate working capital allows wholesalers to seize opportunities that arise where quick financing may be necessary.
5. Maintaining Operational Efficiency: Effective working capital management ensures that wholesalers have sufficient resources to maintain efficient operations, leading to better customer satisfaction and increased profitability.

Techniques for Efficient Working Capital Management:
Here are five techniques real estate wholesalers can utilize for efficient working capital management:
1. Cash Management: Investing excess cash wisely, monitoring expenses, and maintaining a cash reserve for unforeseen circumstances can help businesses better manage their working capital.

2. Receivable Management: Managing accounts receivable more efficiently to collect payments in a timely and orderly fashion can significantly enhance cash flows.

3. Inventory Management: Maintaining inventory levels is essential. Staying cautious of excess inventory avoids obsolescence and increases profitability by reducing associated costs.

4. Payable Management: Efficient vendor management, better negotiation, and vendor consolidation can manage payables more effectively, thus increasing the cash reserve and reducing overburden on working capital.

5. Access to Financing Alternatives: In the case of expansion or an unexpected downturn, having access to financing alternatives such as short-term loans, lines of credit, or factoring can help businesses maintain sufficient working capital.

Effective management of working capital enables wholesalers to run their day-to-day activities without any disruptions. The fundamental purpose of working capital is to ensure sufficient liquidity to meet short-term obligations. Adopting efficient working capital management techniques can go a long way in ensuring sustained growth and long-term success in real estate wholesaling.

Financial Controls:

Financial controls are essential processes and procedures implemented by organizations to ensure the proper management and safeguarding of their financial resources. Two important aspects of financial controls are implementing internal controls to safeguard assets and conducting regular financial audits and reviews. Let's explore these in more detail:

Implementing Internal Controls to Safeguard Assets:
1. Segregation of Duties: Organizations should assign different responsibilities to different individuals to ensure checks and balances. This helps prevent fraud and errors by ensuring that no single person has complete control over financial transactions.
2. Authorization and Approval Processes: Implementing a system of authorization and approval for financial transactions helps ensure that expenditures are properly authorized and within established limits, reducing the risk of unauthorized or fraudulent activities.
3. Physical Security Measures: Organizations should implement physical controls to protect their assets. This includes secure storage of cash, restricted access to financial records, and the use of security systems to prevent unauthorized access.
4. Proper Documentation and Record-Keeping: Maintaining accurate and complete financial records is crucial. This includes properly documenting all transactions, maintaining supporting documents, and recording them in a systematic and organized manner.
5. Regular Reconciliation and Monitoring: Regularly reconciling financial accounts and conducting periodic audits can help identify discrepancies or irregularities. This allows organizations to take corrective measures promptly and ensures the accuracy and reliability of financial data.

Regular Financial Audits and Reviews:
1. External Audits: Organizations may engage external auditors to conduct independent reviews of their financial statements and internal controls. These audits provide an objective assessment of the organization's financial health and the effectiveness of its internal control systems.
2. Internal Audits: Internal audit teams within organizations perform regular reviews of financial processes and controls. This helps identify areas of weakness or improvement, ensuring compliance with policies and regulations.
3. Risk Assessment: Regular financial audits and reviews enable organizations to assess and mitigate risks associated with financial operations. This includes identifying potential fraud risks, evaluating

control weaknesses, and implementing measures to mitigate these risks.
4. Compliance Monitoring: Regular audits and reviews help ensure compliance with laws, regulations, and internal policies. It helps organizations identify any non-compliance issues and take corrective actions to align with legal and regulatory requirements.

By implementing effective internal controls and conducting regular financial audits and reviews, organizations can mitigate risks, prevent fraud, ensure compliance, and safeguard their financial assets. These measures contribute to the financial stability and integrity of the organization.

Using Financial Data for Strategic Decision-Making:

Interpreting Financial Data for Long-Term Strategic Planning:
1. Financial Ratios: Financial ratios provide insights into an organization's financial performance and help assess its financial health. Ratios such as profitability ratios, liquidity ratios, and solvency ratios can be analyzed to understand the organization's strengths and weaknesses and make informed decisions for long-term planning.
2. Trend Analysis: Analyzing financial data over time helps identify trends and patterns. This analysis allows organizations to identify areas of growth, decline, or stability. By understanding these trends, organizations can formulate strategies to capitalize on opportunities and mitigate risks.
3. Comparative Analysis: Comparing financial data with industry benchmarks or competitors' performance helps assess the organization's relative position. This analysis can highlight areas where the organization is performing well or areas that need improvement. It enables organizations to set realistic goals and make informed decisions based on industry standards.
4. Cash Flow Analysis: Analyzing the organization's cash flow is crucial for long-term strategic planning. It helps identify the sources and uses

of cash, assess the organization's ability to meet financial obligations, and plan for investments, expansion, or debt reduction.
5. Scenario Analysis and Sensitivity Analysis: Utilizing financial data for scenario and sensitivity analysis allows organizations to assess the potential impact of different scenarios or changes in key variables. This helps in evaluating the risks and benefits associated with various strategic options.

Case Studies on Successful Financial Management in Real Estate Wholesaling:
1. Efficient Cash Flow Management: A successful real estate wholesaler implemented effective cash flow management by closely monitoring expenses, managing accounts receivable and accounts payable, and optimizing cash utilization. This allowed them to maintain healthy cash reserves and seize investment opportunities.
2. Risk Assessment and Mitigation: Another case study showcased the importance of comprehensive risk assessment and mitigation strategies. By identifying potential risks, such as market fluctuations, regulatory changes, or liquidity issues, the wholesaler implemented risk management strategies, including diversification of investments and maintaining contingency funds.
3. Data-Driven Decision Making: A real estate wholesaler successfully used financial data to drive decision-making processes. They leveraged accurate financial information to evaluate property acquisitions, negotiate deals, and determine optimal pricing strategies. This data-driven approach enabled them to make informed decisions, resulting in profitable outcomes.
4. Strategic Budgeting and Forecasting: Successful wholesalers emphasized the importance of strategic budgeting and forecasting. By accurately projecting revenues, expenses, and cash flows, they could effectively allocate resources, identify areas for cost savings, and plan for future growth and expansion.

These case studies highlight the significance of leveraging financial data for strategic decision-making in real estate wholesaling. By incorporating financial insights into long-term planning, wholesalers can optimize their operations, minimize risks, and achieve sustainable growth.

Conclusion:

In conclusion, effective cash flow management and financial operations are vital for the stability and growth of any business. By summarizing the importance of these aspects, we can understand their significance and the need for continual assessment and improvement.

Cash flow management ensures that an organization has sufficient funds to cover expenses, invest in growth opportunities, and meet financial obligations. It helps maintain liquidity, reduces reliance on external financing, and provides a buffer during unforeseen circumstances. Regular assessment of cash flow enables businesses to identify cash flow gaps, optimize cash utilization, and make informed decisions for long-term sustainability.

Financial operations management encompasses various practices, including budgeting, cost control, financial reporting, and internal controls. These processes ensure the organization's financial health is monitored, risks are mitigated, and compliance with regulations is maintained. Regular assessment of financial practices helps identify areas for improvement, enhances operational efficiency, and strengthens the organization's overall financial management.

Continually assessing and improving financial practices is crucial for business stability and growth. It allows organizations to adapt to market changes, seize new opportunities, and mitigate risks. By staying updated with industry benchmarks, technological advancements, and evolving regulations, businesses can enhance their competitiveness and stay ahead in the market.

In conclusion, businesses should prioritize cash flow management and continually assess and improve their financial practices. By doing so, they can achieve stability, make informed decisions, and foster long-term growth. With a strong foundation in financial operations, businesses can navigate challenges and capitalize on opportunities, ensuring their sustained success in the dynamic business landscape.

Part IV: Development and Networking

Development and networking are two essential aspects that go hand in hand in various professional fields. In this context, development refers to personal and professional growth, while networking refers to building valuable connections and relationships with others in your industry or field of interest. The combination of development and networking can have a significant impact on career advancement, knowledge acquisition, and overall success.

Development involves continuous learning, skill enhancement, and personal growth. It encompasses various activities such as attending workshops, pursuing higher education, acquiring new certifications, and honing existing skills. Development allows individuals to stay updated with industry trends, broaden their knowledge base, and adapt to changing scenarios. By investing in development, individuals position themselves as knowledgeable and skilled professionals who can contribute effectively and adapt to dynamic environments.

Networking, on the other hand, is the process of building and nurturing relationships with others in your professional sphere. Through networking, individuals can establish connections with colleagues, industry experts, potential mentors, and influential individuals. Networking offers opportunities for collaboration, knowledge sharing, and access to resources that can propel one's career forward. It also provides a platform for professional support, guidance, and exposure to diverse perspectives and experiences.

The symbiotic relationship between development and networking is evident. Development supports networking by providing individuals with the necessary knowledge, skills, and expertise to contribute meaningfully to professional interactions. Networking, in turn, enhances development by facilitating access to valuable resources, learning opportunities, and exposure to different viewpoints.

Combining development and networking is a strategic approach for career growth. By actively seeking out developmental opportunities and fostering meaningful connections, individuals can expand their professional horizons, unlock new possibilities, and stay relevant in their respective fields. The integration of development and networking is particularly valuable in today's interconnected world, where collaboration and knowledge sharing are vital for success.

In conclusion, development and networking are two interconnected processes that play a vital role in professional growth and success. By pursuing continuous development and actively engaging in networking activities, individuals can create a powerful synergy that propels their careers forward, enables lifelong learning, and opens doors to new opportunities.

Chapter 7: Building a Robust Professional Network

Networking in Real Estate Wholesaling

In the world of real estate wholesaling, building a strong professional network is not just beneficial—it's crucial for success. The power of networking extends far beyond simple social connections; it opens doors to business opportunities, enhances knowledge sharing, and establishes a foundation for long-lasting relationships. In this chapter, we will explore the importance of a professional network in real estate wholesaling and highlight the specific benefits of networking within the real estate industry.

Real estate wholesaling, for those unfamiliar, is a unique investment strategy that involves finding deeply discounted properties and assigning the purchase contract to another buyer for a fee. It requires extensive knowledge of the market, effective marketing strategies, and most importantly, a vast network of industry professionals.

So, why is a professional network so vital in the realm of real estate wholesaling? Let's dive deeper into the reasons:

1. Access to Off-Market Deals: In the competitive real estate market, access to off-market properties gives wholesalers a significant advantage. These properties are not publicly listed and are often discovered through networking channels. With a solid professional network, wholesalers gain access to a hidden market of motivated sellers, distressed properties, and pre-foreclosure opportunities. This access allows them to source highly lucrative deals that may not be available to the general public.

2. Reliable Sources of Funding: Real estate wholesaling requires quick and efficient transactions, often involving cash offers. Building strong relationships with investors, private lenders, and hard money lenders can provide wholesalers with a reliable source of funding for their deals. Through networking, they can connect with individuals or organizations willing to invest in their projects, negotiate favorable terms, and secure the necessary capital.

3. Partnering with Experienced Investors: Collaborating with experienced investors can be a game-changer in real estate wholesaling. By networking with seasoned professionals, wholesalers can tap into their knowledge, expertise, and resources. This collaboration can help them navigate the complexities of the market, gain insights into deal analysis, and learn effective negotiation strategies. Partnering with experienced investors also creates opportunities for joint ventures, increasing deal flow and profit potential.

4. Access to Supportive Services: Real estate wholesaling involves various tasks that go beyond finding and assigning contracts. Wholesalers need access to a range of supportive services, such as attorneys, title companies, contractors, photographers, and property managers. Building a network of reliable and trustworthy service providers can streamline the wholesaling process, ensuring smooth transactions, and minimizing complications.

5. Knowledge Sharing and Education: An effective professional network provides opportunities for continuous learning and growth. Networking events, conferences, and online communities bring together like-minded individuals, creating an environment for knowledge sharing, brainstorming ideas, and staying informed about industry trends. By engaging with others in the real estate community, wholesalers can stay up to date with market developments, learn from experts, and adapt their strategies accordingly.

Networking benefits specific to the real estate industry span beyond just business opportunities. They foster a sense of community, support, and collaboration. Wholesalers can gain friendships, mentors, and valuable connections that enrich their personal and professional lives. Additionally, networking allows wholesalers to stay motivated, inspired, and accountable as they interact with others who share their passion for real estate.

In conclusion, a robust professional network is of utmost importance in the field of real estate wholesaling. It opens doors to off-market deals, provides access to reliable funding, facilitates partnerships with experienced investors, connects wholesalers with essential services, and fosters knowledge sharing. By actively building and nurturing their network, wholesalers position themselves for long-term success in this dynamic and competitive industry.

So, let's put the power of networking into action and harness its benefits to propel ourselves forward in the world of real estate wholesaling.

Identifying Key Relationships in Real Estate Wholesaling

When it comes to building a successful real estate wholesaling business, it is essential to identify and cultivate key relationships. These relationships encompass various individuals and professional contacts who play critical roles in your business success. By understanding the importance and distinct roles of each contact, you can effectively leverage their expertise, resources, and support to propel your wholesaling endeavors. In this section, we will explore how to identify and categorize essential contacts in the real estate industry, along with the roles they play in your business success.

1. Investors: Investors are the lifeblood of real estate wholesaling. They provide the necessary capital to finance your deals and enable you to secure properties quickly. These contacts may include individual investors, private equity firms, hedge funds, or other financial institutions. Building relationships with investors is crucial as they can offer valuable funding resources, guidance in analyzing deals, and a network of potential buyers. Additionally, investors may also be interested in forming joint ventures, where they provide the funds while wholesalers bring deals and local market knowledge to the table.

2. Real Estate Agents: Real estate agents are invaluable contacts in wholesaling. They have access to the Multiple Listing Service (MLS)

and can help you identify potential properties in your target market. Developing collaborative relationships with real estate agents can lead to off-market opportunities, as they may come across distressed or undervalued properties in their network. Agents can also guide you through the process of submitting offers, negotiating contracts, and navigating legal complexities. Establishing a rapport with agents who understand your investment strategy and goals can streamline property acquisitions and boost your deal flow.

3. Contractors and Rehab Specialists: Reliable and skilled contractors are vital for successfully executing property renovations or repairs. Many wholesale deals require some level of rehab work to maximize the property's value and attractiveness to potential buyers. Having a network of trusted contractors and rehab specialists ensures that you can quickly obtain accurate cost estimates, complete renovations in a timely manner, and avoid unnecessary complications. These contacts can help you assess the scope of work needed, recommend cost-effective solutions, and execute the necessary improvements to increase the property's marketability.

4. Legal Advisors: Real estate transactions involve various legal intricacies and contracts, making legal advisors indispensable partners in wholesaling. These contacts may include real estate attorneys or specialized lawyers familiar with real estate and investment laws. Legal advisors can assist you in structuring contracts, ensuring compliance with local regulations, and mitigating any legal risks. Understanding the legal aspects of wholesaling, such as assigning contracts and navigating specific market regulations, is critical to protecting your interests and maintaining ethical business practices.

5. Title Companies and Escrow Agents: Title companies and escrow agents are essential for the smooth transfer of property ownership during wholesale transactions. These contacts facilitate the closing process, ensuring that all necessary documents and funds are

handled securely and accurately. Working with reputable title companies and escrow agents helps ensure that each transaction is completed legally and efficiently. They handle details such as title searches, preparing closing documents, and disbursing funds, allowing you to focus on sourcing and assigning contracts.

6. Real Estate Networks and Associations: Engaging with real estate networks and industry associations can provide access to a wide range of contacts, knowledge, and resources. Joining local real estate investor groups, attending industry conferences, or participating in online forums allows you to connect with like-minded professionals, share insights, and expand your network. Being part of these networks offers opportunities to learn from experienced wholesalers, gain exposure to new strategies, and stay abreast of market trends.

Understanding the unique roles each contact plays in your real estate wholesaling business is crucial. Identifying and categorizing essential contacts from investors to contractors, legal advisors, real estate agents, and more, ensures that you can leverage their specific expertise, resources, and support for your success. Developing and nurturing these relationships requires proactive networking, effective communication, and cultivating mutual trust. By strategically building your network, you will create a foundation for long-term success in the dynamic world of real estate wholesaling.

Strategies for Networking in Real Estate Wholesaling

Networking plays a pivotal role in the success of real estate wholesaling. It allows you to meet and connect with industry professionals who can provide valuable insights, opportunities, and support. In this section, we will explore key strategies for effectively networking in the real estate industry and offer tips for maintaining and nurturing professional relationships.

1. Attend Real Estate Networking Events: Real estate networking events, such as conferences, seminars, and meetups, are excellent opportunities to meet like-minded professionals and expand your network. These events often feature speakers, panel discussions, and breakout sessions that provide valuable insights and industry trends. Actively engage with other attendees, exchange business cards, and follow up with personalized messages after the event. Remember, networking is not only about collecting contacts but building authentic relationships.

2. Join Online Real Estate Communities: Online forums, social media groups, and real estate-specific platforms provide virtual spaces for networking in the digital realm. Join active and reputable communities where wholesalers, investors, agents, and other industry professionals gather. Participate in discussions, share insights, and offer support to others. By demonstrating your expertise and actively engaging with the community, you can attract potential collaborators, investors, and mentors.

3. Leverage Local Real Estate Investor Groups: Local real estate investor groups are valuable resources for connecting with professionals in your area. These groups often organize regular meetings, property tours, or educational sessions. Attend these local gatherings to meet wholesalers, investors, agents, and other individuals directly involved in the local market. Utilize these opportunities to build relationships, share experiences, and learn from each other.

4. Utilize Social Media Platforms: Social media platforms like LinkedIn, Facebook, and Instagram can be powerful tools for networking. Create a professional online presence, share relevant content, and connect with industry professionals in your target market. Engage in conversations, offer insights, and showcase your expertise. Actively follow and connect with influential individuals in the real estate

industry to stay updated on market trends and potentially collaborate on future deals.

5. Offer Value and Build Relationships: Networking is not just about what you can gain; it's also about what you can offer. Be generous with your knowledge, share helpful resources, and provide support to others in your network. By offering value to your contacts, you build trust and position yourself as a valuable resource. This can lead to referrals, joint ventures, and long-term professional relationships.

Tips for Maintaining and Nurturing Professional Relationships:

1. Regularly Follow Up: After meeting someone at an event or exchanging contact information, it's crucial to follow up in a timely manner. Send personalized messages to express gratitude, reference specific conversations, or offer assistance. Regularly checking in with your contacts helps maintain the connection and keeps you top of mind when opportunities arise.

2. Stay Engaged: Networking is an ongoing process, so it's essential to stay engaged with your contacts. Interact with them on social media platforms, comment on their posts, and congratulate them on their achievements. Attend industry events or meetups where you can reconnect face-to-face. Show genuine interest in their projects and offer support when needed.

3. Seek Mutual Benefits: Networking is a give-and-take process. Look for ways to provide value to your contacts and seek opportunities for collaboration or mutual benefits. Share relevant industry information, refer clients or investors to contacts when appropriate, and explore potential joint ventures that can benefit both parties.

4. Personalize Communication: When reaching out to your contacts, personalize your messages to make them feel valued. Reference specific conversations or projects you discussed, mention shared

interests, or congratulate them on their accomplishments. Personalized communication shows that you genuinely care and strengthens the bond between you and your contacts.

5. Attend Industry Conferences and Events: Regularly attending industry conferences and events allows you to reconnect with old contacts while also expanding your network. Take advantage of opportunities to meet new professionals, attend workshops, and engage in panel discussions. By consistently attending such events, you demonstrate your commitment to professional growth and networking.

In conclusion, these networking strategies and nurturing professional relationships, you can foster a strong and supportive network within the real estate wholesaling industry. Remember, networking is not just about expanding your contact list, but about building lasting connections with individuals who can contribute to your success and vice versa. Focus on creating mutually beneficial relationships that can open doors to new opportunities and propel your real estate wholesaling business forward.

Attending Industry Events and Conferences for Real Estate Networking

Industry events and conferences are excellent opportunities for real estate professionals to network, learn from industry experts, and stay updated on the latest trends and developments. In this section, we will explore strategies to get the most out of real estate events, seminars, and conferences, as well as effective follow-up strategies to solidify new connections.

1. Preparing for the Event:

- Research the Event: Before attending, thoroughly research the event to understand the agenda, speakers, and topics being covered. Identify sessions, workshops, or panels that align with your interests and goals.

- Set Clear Objectives: Define your goals for attending the event. Are you looking to network, gain industry knowledge, or find new business opportunities? Setting clear objectives will help you prioritize your time and efforts.

- Prepare Your Materials: Bring an ample supply of business cards to exchange with fellow attendees. Consider having a concise and compelling elevator pitch ready to introduce yourself and your real estate endeavors.

2. Active Networking at the Event:

- Engage in Conversations: Take the initiative to approach other attendees during breaks or networking sessions. Ask open-ended questions, actively listen, and show genuine interest in their work and experiences.

- Attend Social Events: Many industry events include social events like cocktail parties or networking dinners. Take advantage of these opportunities to connect with professionals in a more relaxed and informal setting.

- Utilize Social Media: Use event-specific hashtags or geotags on social media platforms to connect with fellow attendees. Share insights, photos, or interesting moments from the event and engage in discussions online.

3. Maximizing Learning Opportunities:

- Attend Relevant Sessions: Prioritize attending sessions that align with your interests and goals. Take notes and actively participate by asking questions during Q&A sessions.

- Network with Speakers: Approach speakers after their sessions to introduce yourself, ask specific questions, or share your thoughts on their presentation. Speakers are often open to networking and can provide valuable insights or future collaboration opportunities.

4. Effective Follow-Up:

- Organize Contact Information: After the event, organize the business cards or contact information you collected. Add relevant notes to remember key details about each connection.

- Personalized Follow-Up: Within a few days of the event, send personalized follow-up messages or emails to the individuals you met. Reference specific conversations, topics discussed, or shared interests to demonstrate your attentiveness and genuine interest.

- Connect on LinkedIn: Expand your online network by connecting with your new contacts on LinkedIn. Personalize your connection requests by mentioning where you met and expressing your interest in staying connected.

- Provide Value: Offer to share relevant resources, industry articles, or insights that may be of interest to your new connections. Providing value strengthens the connection and shows your willingness to support and contribute.

- Schedule Follow-Up Meetings: If you believe there is potential for collaboration or a further business discussion, propose a follow-up meeting or call. This allows you to deepen the connection and explore potential synergies.

- Stay in Touch: Remember to nurture the relationships beyond the initial follow-up. Engage with your connections on social media, comment on their posts, and maintain periodic check-ins to keep the relationship alive.

By following these strategies, you can make the most out of real estate events and conferences, forge new connections, expand your network, and stay ahead of industry trends. Remember, successful networking doesn't end with the event itself; it requires consistent effort, personalized follow-up, and ongoing engagement to solidify and cultivate valuable professional relationships.

Creating Value in Relationships for Real Estate Networking

Building strong and meaningful relationships is crucial in the real estate industry. To foster long-lasting connections, it is important to provide value to your network contacts and embrace the principle of reciprocity. In this section, we will explore the importance of reciprocity in professional relationships and provide examples of how you can create value for your network contacts.

1. Importance of Reciprocity:

Reciprocity is at the core of successful networking. It is the principle of mutual exchange and benefits where both parties contribute and receive value. By offering assistance, support, and resources to others, you establish a foundation for fruitful long-term relationships. Here's why reciprocity is important:

- Trust and Credibility: Providing value and support to others helps build trust and credibility. When you demonstrate your willingness to help, you establish yourself as a reliable and trustworthy professional.

- Relationship Building: Reciprocity strengthens relationships by creating a sense of mutual respect and appreciation. As you offer value, you deepen the connection and foster a positive rapport with others.

- Opportunities for Collaboration: When you create value for others, you open doors for potential collaborations. By contributing your knowledge, resources, or expertise, you encourage reciprocity from others who may offer similar support or opportunities in return.

2. Examples of Providing Value to Your Network Contacts:

- Sharing Industry Insights: Share relevant and valuable industry insights through articles, blog posts, or social media updates. This helps keep your connections informed and positions you as a knowledgeable resource.

- Introductions and Referrals: Connect people in your network who could benefit from each other's services or expertise. Introduce colleagues, clients, or partners who can create mutually beneficial relationships.

- Offering Expertise: Provide advice, guidance, or mentorship to individuals who are looking for real estate insights or facing challenges in their professional journeys. Share your knowledge and experiences to support their growth.

- Providing Resources: Share useful resources such as templates, market reports, or tools that can assist your network contacts in their business endeavors. Be proactive in identifying and sharing valuable resources that can benefit them.

- Celebrating Achievements: Acknowledge and celebrate the accomplishments and milestones of your network contacts. Congratulate them publicly on social media, send personalized notes, or attend their events to show your support.

- Facilitating Learning Opportunities: Share details about educational programs, webinars, or conferences that could be valuable to your network connections. Help them expand their knowledge and skills by giving them access to valuable learning opportunities.

- Actively Engaging: Like, comment, and share your connections' content on social media platforms to boost their visibility and show your support. Engage in conversations, ask questions, and be a proactive participant in their online discussions.

Remember, creating value in relationships is not about keeping score or expecting immediate returns. It is about genuinely helping others and fostering a culture of mutual support. By embracing the principle of reciprocity and consistently offering value to your network contacts, you can nurture strong relationships that can lead to collaborative opportunities, referrals, and long-term success in the real estate industry.

Local Real Estate Groups and Associations for Networking

Joining local real estate investment groups and professional associations can offer a range of benefits to real estate professionals. In this section, we will explore the advantages of joining these groups and how active participation can expand your network and enhance your credibility.

1. Benefits of Joining Local Real Estate Groups and Associations:

- Networking Opportunities: Local real estate groups and associations provide a platform to connect with like-minded professionals, including investors, agents, brokers, property managers, and industry experts. Networking within these communities can lead to collaboration, referrals, and valuable insights.

- Knowledge Sharing and Learning: These groups often offer educational events, workshops, and seminars where members can gain valuable industry knowledge. By attending these events, you can enhance your understanding of real estate trends, strategies, and best practices.

- Access to Resources: Local real estate groups and associations typically provide access to a wide range of resources like market reports, industry publications, legal updates, and research materials. These resources can help you stay updated with the latest industry developments.

- Collaboration Opportunities: Joining these groups allows you to find potential partners or team members for real estate projects. By connecting with professionals who share similar objectives, you can explore collaboration opportunities and expand your business ventures.

- Advocacy and Representation: Many associations actively advocate for the real estate industry's interests and rights. By becoming a member, you contribute to the collective voice of the industry and support initiatives that benefit real estate professionals as a whole.

2. How Active Participation Expands Your Network and Credibility:

- Engage in Networking Events: Attend networking events organized by these groups to meet fellow members, share experiences, and exchange ideas. Actively participate in discussions, ask questions, and offer insights to demonstrate your expertise and eagerness to connect.

- Volunteer for Committees or Leadership Roles: Take on active roles within these groups, such as joining committees or pursuing leadership positions. This involvement not only expands your network but also showcases your commitment to the industry and your willingness to contribute.

- Share Your Expertise: Offer to present on topics you specialize in at group events or participate in panel discussions. Sharing your knowledge and experiences positions you as a credible professional and helps you build your personal brand.

- Collaborate on Projects: Actively seek opportunities to collaborate with other members on real estate projects. By working together, you can showcase your skills, strengthen relationships, and create valuable outcomes.

- Contribute to Group Discussions: Engage in online forums, social media groups, and mailing lists to share valuable insights, answer questions, and contribute to discussions. This establishes your credibility and expertise within the community.

- Attend Educational Programs: Make the most of educational programs offered by these groups, such as seminars or workshops. By actively participating in learning opportunities, you not only expand your knowledge but also showcase your commitment to professional growth and improvement.

- Stay Updated and Engaged: Regularly check group updates, newsletters, and publications to stay informed about industry news, events, and opportunities. Engage with fellow members by commenting on their posts and contributing to discussions, demonstrating your active involvement.

By joining local real estate groups and associations and actively participating in their activities, you can expand your network, gain valuable knowledge, and enhance your credibility within the industry. Remember, the key to benefiting from these opportunities lies in active engagement, genuine interest in others, and a willingness to contribute to the community.

Conclusion:

Building and maintaining a professional network is of strategic importance in the real estate industry. Throughout this discussion, we have highlighted the key reasons why networking is crucial and provided insights into effective networking strategies. Let's recap the strategic importance of building and maintaining a professional network and encourage you to proactively engage with and expand your professional circle:

1. Strategic Importance of Building and Maintaining a Professional Network:

- Access to Opportunities: Networking provides access to a wide range of opportunities, including referrals, partnerships, joint ventures, and shared knowledge. By cultivating a strong network, you can increase your chances of finding new clients, projects, and collaborations.

- Industry Knowledge and Insights: Engaging with professionals in your field allows you to tap into a vast pool of knowledge and insights. By building relationships with industry leaders and peers, you can stay updated on market trends, best practices, and innovative strategies.

- Support and Mentoring: A professional network can provide valuable support and mentoring opportunities. Engaging with experienced individuals who have faced similar challenges can offer guidance, motivation, and encouragement throughout your career.

- Credibility and Reputation: Building a network of respected professionals can enhance your credibility and reputation. When others trust and endorse you, it can positively impact your business and attract new clients or partners.

2. Encouragement to Proactively Engage with and Expand Your Professional Circle:

- Be Proactive: Don't wait for networking opportunities to come your way – take the initiative to engage proactively. Attend industry events, join relevant associations, and participate in online communities. Put yourself out there and seize opportunities to connect with others.

- Nurture Relationships: Building a strong network is not just about making connections; it's about cultivating meaningful relationships. Invest time and effort in nurturing relationships with your network contacts. Follow up regularly, offer your support, and provide value whenever possible.

- Embrace Diversity: Seek to expand the diversity of your professional circle. Connect with professionals from different backgrounds, industries, and perspectives. This can bring fresh insights, widen your knowledge base, and open doors to new opportunities.

- Give and Receive: Remember that networking is a reciprocal process. Be willing to offer assistance, insights, and resources to others in your network. Actively contribute to their success, and you will find that opportunities and support will flow back to you.

- Be Genuine: Authenticity is key in building strong professional relationships. Be genuine in your interactions, show interest in others, and listen actively. Building trust and rapport can lead to long-term fruitful connections.

In conclusion, building and maintaining a professional network is essential for success in the real estate industry. It provides access to opportunities, industry knowledge, support, and helps to enhance your credibility. So, take the initiative to engage proactively, nurture relationships, embrace diversity, and remember to give and receive. By actively and authentically expanding your professional circle, you can unlock limitless potential and achieve greater success in your real estate career.

Chapter 8: Working with Real Estate Agents and Other Professionals

Collaborating with real estate agents and other professionals is essential for anyone involved in the real estate market. Whether you are a buyer, seller, investor, or even a real estate professional yourself, working alongside experienced professionals can provide you with numerous benefits.

Importance of collaborating with real estate agents and other professionals: Collaborating with real estate agents and other professionals is crucial because it allows you to tap into their expertise and experience. Real estate agents possess in-depth knowledge about the local market, pricing trends, and property values. Their expertise can help you make informed decisions and navigate the complexities of buying or selling a property.

Additionally, collaborating with other professionals such as mortgage brokers, lawyers, home inspectors, and appraisers can further enhance your real estate journey. These professionals bring specialized knowledge to the table and can guide you through the legal, financial, and technical aspects of the transaction.

Benefits of leveraging expert knowledge and networks:
One of the primary benefits of collaborating with real estate agents and other professionals is their extensive network. These professionals have built relationships with other industry experts, including fellow agents, mortgage lenders, contractors, and more. Leveraging their network can open doors to opportunities that you might not have otherwise encountered.

Furthermore, real estate professionals have a broad understanding of the market, including upcoming developments, investment opportunities, and potential pitfalls. By leveraging their expert knowledge, you can gain valuable insights and make strategic decisions.

Collaborating with professionals also gives you access to their resources, including market research data, negotiation skills, and marketing strategies. This can save you time, effort, and potential financial setbacks by ensuring that you make well-informed decisions.

In summary, collaborating with real estate agents and other professionals is vital for maximizing your chances of success in the real estate market. Their expertise, network, and resources can provide you with a competitive advantage and help you achieve your real estate goals.

What would you like to explore further or add to this chapter on working with real estate agents and other professionals?.

Roles of Real Estate Agents in Wholesaling:

Real estate agents play a crucial role in the wholesaling process, acting as intermediaries between buyers and sellers. Their expertise, industry knowledge, and network connections make them valuable assets in facilitating successful wholesale transactions. Let's delve into the specific roles they play:

1. Facilitating Deal Sourcing: Real estate agents have access to multiple listing services (MLS) and various databases, which grant them a comprehensive view of available properties. They actively search for potential wholesale deals and identify properties with significant potential for investors. This enables them to notify their clients about lucrative opportunities promptly. By leveraging their market knowledge, agents can match the needs and preferences of their investor clients with suitable wholesale properties.

2. Conducting Market Analysis: Real estate agents analyze market trends, property values, and comparable sales to determine the potential profitability of a wholesaling opportunity. They provide valuable insights to investors regarding property condition, market demand, and potential resale value. By thoroughly understanding the local market, agents help investors make informed decisions and mitigate risks.

3. Negotiating Purchase Contracts: Agents specialize in negotiations and are skilled at securing favorable terms for their clients. In wholesaling, agents negotiate purchase contracts with sellers on behalf of the investor. They ensure that the contract includes favorable pricing and terms, such as an appropriate inspection period and contingencies. Skilled agents strive to create a win-win situation for both the investor and the seller, ensuring a smooth transaction process.

4. Assisting with Due Diligence: Real estate agents aid in conducting due diligence on wholesale properties. They coordinate inspections, obtain property disclosures, and review relevant documents. This thorough due diligence ensures that investors have a clear understanding of the property's condition and potential challenges before finalizing the deal.

Understanding the Legal and Ethical Duties of Real Estate Agents:

Alongside their roles, real estate agents have legal and ethical obligations that must be adhered to. This ensures transparency, fairness, and protection for all parties involved:

1. Fiduciary Duty: Real estate agents owe their clients a fiduciary duty, which means they must act in the best interests of their clients, putting their clients' needs above their own. This duty encompasses loyalty, confidentiality, accountability, and full disclosure of material facts.

2. Honest and Fair Representation: Agents must provide accurate and truthful information to clients about the property, market conditions, and any potential risks associated with the transaction. They should refrain from misrepresentation, omitting material facts, or engaging in any deceptive practices.

3. Compliance with Laws and Regulations: Real estate agents are obligated to comply with all applicable laws and regulations in their jurisdiction. This includes fair housing laws, disclosure requirements, and any specific guidelines related to wholesaling or real estate transactions.

4. Confidentiality: Agents are entrusted with sensitive information during the transaction process. They must maintain the confidentiality of their clients' personal and financial details, only sharing information with authorized parties or as required by law.

5. Professionalism and Integrity: Real estate agents are expected to uphold high standards of professionalism and integrity. They should conduct themselves ethically, treat all parties involved with respect, and refrain from engaging in any activities that could compromise their clients' interests or reputation.

By understanding these legal and ethical duties, both investors and sellers can ensure that they are working with trustworthy and reliable real estate agents.

In conclusion, real estate agents play essential roles in wholesaling by facilitating deal sourcing and negotiations. Their expertise in market analysis, contract negotiation, and due diligence ensures a smooth and successful transaction process. Furthermore, adhering to legal and ethical duties is key in maintaining trust and ensuring transparency in the wholesaling industry.

Choosing the Right Real Estate Agent for Wholesaling:

When it comes to wholesaling real estate, having a skilled and experienced real estate agent on your side can make a significant difference in the success of your transactions. Here are some criteria and considerations for selecting the right agent:

1. Experience in Wholesaling: Look for an agent who has specific experience in wholesaling. Wholesaling involves a unique set of skills and strategies that may differ from traditional real estate transactions. An agent who has successfully completed wholesale deals in the past will be familiar with the intricacies of the process, understand the investor's perspective, and possess the necessary negotiation skills to secure favorable terms.

2. Local Market Expertise: Choose an agent who has a deep understanding of the local market where you plan to conduct wholesaling deals. They should be knowledgeable about the neighborhoods, property values, market trends, and potential investment opportunities. This understanding will enable them to identify profitable wholesale properties and provide accurate guidance on pricing and market conditions.

3. Extensive Network: An agent with a strong network in the real estate industry can be a valuable asset. They should have connections with other investors, property wholesalers, contractors, and professionals such as attorneys and inspectors. This network can provide access to off-market deals and additional resources that may be necessary for successful wholesaling transactions.

4. Communication and Responsiveness: Effective communication is crucial in wholesaling. Look for an agent who is accessible and responsive to your inquiries and needs. They should be proactive in keeping you updated on potential deals, responding to emails and

phone calls promptly, and maintaining open lines of communication throughout the entire transaction process.

5. Professionalism and Integrity: Choose an agent who demonstrates professionalism and operates with integrity. They should adhere to ethical standards, follow legal requirements, and act in your best interest. Look for positive reviews or references from previous clients to ensure that the agent has a track record of professionalism and ethical conduct.

Interview Questions to Assess Agent Capabilities and Compatibility:

Once you've identified potential agents, conducting interviews can help you assess their capabilities and determine if they are the right fit for your wholesaling needs. Here are some interview questions to consider:

1. How familiar are you with the wholesaling process? Have you successfully completed wholesale deals in the past?
2. Can you provide references from clients you have worked within wholesaling transactions?
3. What is your approach to sourcing potential wholesale deals? How do you find off-market properties?
4. How do you analyze market trends and determine the potential profitability of a wholesale property?
5. How do you negotiate purchase contracts? Can you provide an example of a successful negotiation you have conducted in the past?
6. How do you handle due diligence and ensure that all necessary inspections and paperwork are completed accurately and on time?
7. How do you communicate with your clients throughout the transaction process? How frequently can I expect updates from you?
8. Can you explain your network of industry contacts and how it can benefit my wholesaling endeavors?
9. How do you handle conflicts of interest or potential ethical dilemmas that may arise during the wholesaling process?

10. Have you ever faced any legal or ethical issues in your real estate career, and how did you handle them?

Remember to not only assess their technical capabilities but also evaluate their compatibility with your working style and goals. Trust your instincts and choose an agent whom you feel comfortable working with and who aligns with your values and objectives.

In conclusion, selecting the right real estate agent for wholesaling involves considering their experience in wholesaling, local market expertise, network connections, communication skills, professionalism, and integrity. Conducting thorough interviews with potential agents will help you assess their capabilities and compatibility.

Working with Contractors for Property Sale Preparation:

When it comes to preparing a property for sale, a skilled and experienced contractor can help optimize its value and appeal to potential buyers. From home repairs to renovations, the right contractor can make all the difference. Here are some ways a contractor can support you when preparing a property for sale:

1. Property Inspection: A professional inspection of the property can identify any necessary repairs or upgrades to boost its value and improve buyer perception. A contractor can help identify these issues and provide advice on how best to address them.

2. Repairs: From minor to major fixes, a contractor can help with repairs that may be required before a sale. They can repair damaged roofs, damaged walls, and floors, repair plumbing issues, and much more.

3. Interior and Exterior Upgrades: Professional contractors can also contribute significantly to upgrading the property's aesthetics and functionality. Contractors can offer advice on paint colors, new tiles, flooring types, and kitchen, and bathroom upgrades. Exterior

upgrades like landscaping, fencing, painting or pressure washing can also improve the property's appeal.

4. Staging: Some contractors provide staging options that help show the property to its best advantage. They can offer designing suggestions and move furniture around to improve the property's aesthetic appeal to potential buyers.

Tips for Finding and Vetting Reliable Contractors:

Finding and vetting a reliable contractor can be a daunting task, with many factors to consider. Below are some tips to help you make an informed choice when selecting a contractor for your property sale:

1. Conduct thorough research.

Check online directories like HomeAdvisor, Yelp, and Angie's List to find qualified contractors in your area. Look for reviews and ratings from clients who have worked with the contractors in the past.

2. Seek recommendations from trusted sources.

Ask friends, family, or acquaintances if they can recommend any contractors whom they have previously worked with. Recommendations can be a valuable resource in finding dependable contractors who have been vetted by someone you trust.

3. Verify credentials.

Ensure that the contractor you select holds a valid license and has necessary certifications. Contacting professional associations like the National Association of the Remodeling Industry (NARI) and the National Association of Home Builders (NAHB) can help you find qualified professionals with the necessary certifications.

4. Ask for references.

Ask for references from the contractor to help you evaluate their past work and ensure client satisfaction. This way, you can assess their work quality, timeliness, and professionalism based on direct feedback from previous clients.

5. Request for details of past projects.

Ask potential contractors for portfolios or examples of their previous work to see whether their style and quality of work align with your preferences and standards.

6. Get multiple quotes.

Request multiple quotes from different contractors. This will help you compare prices and services offered and ensure that you get the best deal without compromising quality.

7. Get everything in writing.

Ensure that you receive a contract with clear details of the job scope, timelines, payment schedules, and any relevant warranties or guarantees. This will help you avoid any misunderstandings and protect you in case of any disputes that may arise.

In conclusion, working with contractors can help the preparation of properties for sale a smooth and successful process. To ensure you find the right contractor, conduct thorough research, seek recommendations, verify credentials, ask for references and project examples, get multiple quotes, and receive a written contract.

Engaging with Legal Professionals for Real Estate Transactions:

Whether you're a buyer, seller, or investor in real estate, legal professionals offer essential guidance and support throughout the transaction process. They can help navigate legal requirements, ensure contractual compliance, and mitigate risks. Here are some reasons why legal advice is necessary in contracts and real estate deals:

1. Legal Compliance:Real estate transactions are subject to local laws and regulations that must be followed to avoid legal complications. A real estate attorney can help ensure that all legal requirements are met and that the transaction is compliant.

2. Contractual Protection:A real estate attorney can help draft or review contracts and agreements to ensure clarity and protect against any potential legal disputes or problems.

3. Risk Mitigation:A real estate attorney can help identify potential risks and liabilities that may arise during the transaction and mitigate those risks.

How to Find and Choose a Real Estate Attorney:

Finding and choosing the right real estate attorney requires some careful consideration and research. Below are some steps to help you select the right legal professional:

1. Conduct Thorough Research: Start by exploring online directories and conducting a preliminary search for lawyers who specialize in real estate. Check their websites and credentials, as well as ratings, and reviews from previous clients.

2. Check the Lawyer's Credentials: Verify the lawyer's credentials and licensure. The lawyer should have a valid license to practice law in your state and be a member of the state bar association.

3. Check the Lawyer's Experience: Choose a lawyer who has extensive experience in real estate law and transactions. Look for their background and areas of expertise as well as their track record of successful real estate transactions.

4. Seek Recommendations: Ask for recommendations from family, friends, or other real estate professionals. People who have worked with lawyers in the past can offer valuable insights and recommendations.

5. Check Availability: A lawyer's availability is critical when it comes to real estate transactions. Ensure that the lawyer can provide the necessary attention you need during the transaction process.

6. Conduct an Interview: Schedule a consultation with the lawyer to discuss your case and evaluate their communication and listening skills to determine their ability to handle your case. Ask about their availability, communication style, and fees to ensure alignment.

7. Understand the Fees: Legal fees vary by type of case and complexity. Understand the lawyer's fee structure and billing methods before engaging the lawyer. This will help you avoid any surprises about legal fees and expenses.

In conclusion, engaging with a legal professional is necessary in real estate transactions to ensure compliance with local laws and regulations, protect against legal disputes, and mitigate risks. To choose the right real estate attorney, conduct thorough research, check credentials and experience, seek recommendations, understand availability and fees, and conduct an interview.

Building Relationships with Financial Experts for Property Investment:

When it comes to property investment, working with an accountant and financial advisor can be valuable in creating a successful investment portfolio that aligns with your financial goals. These professionals can offer expert guidance on financial management, tax planning, and deal structuring. Below are some ways an accountant and financial advisor can help with your real estate investment:

1. Financial Planning: A financial advisor can offer advice on developing a financial plan that aligns with your long-term investment goals. They can help you understand the investment return and create a strategy to manage your assets and risks.

2. Tax Planning: An accountant can advise on tax strategies and help reduce tax liability for your investments. They can help you optimize your tax position during the investment lifecycle, which can save money and improve investment returns.

3. Deal Structuring: A financial advisor can offer expertise in structuring deals and financial structures that align with your investment objectives. They can help develop the right deal structures to minimize risk and maximize returns.

4. Portfolio Management: A financial advisor can help manage and monitor your investment portfolio, optimize asset allocation, monitor performance, and rebalance it to align with your financial objectives.

How to Find and Choose an Accountant and Financial Advisor:

Finding the right accountant and financial advisor can be instrumental in your real estate investment. Here are some steps to help you find and choose the right professionals:

1. Conduct Thorough Research:Start by conducting a thorough search of local professionals online. Check websites, credentials, and past experience, and read reviews, and ratings from previous clients.

2. Check Professional Credentials: Verify that the accountant is a Certified Public Accountant (CPA) or Chartered Accountant (CA) with the necessary credentials to practice accountancy, and the financial advisor is a Certified Financial Planner (CFP) or has the required credentials to practice financial planning.

3. Check Past Experience: Choose professionals with extensive experience in real estate investment and management. Ask for their background and areas of expertise, and verify that they have successfully helped clients with real estate investment in the past.

4. Seek Recommendations: Ask for recommendations from family, friends, or other professionals in the real estate industry. They can provide valuable insights and recommendations based on their experiences.

5. Interview the Professionals: Schedule consultations with the prospective accountant and financial advisor to discuss your needs and determine their ability to help manage your investment portfolio. Ask about their availability, communication style, and fees to ensure alignment.

6. Understand the Fees: Accountants and financial advisors charge differently based on the scope of services provided, the complexity of your portfolio, and the terms of their engagement. Understand the fees and billing methods of the accountant and financial advisor before engaging them to avoid surprises about fees and expenses.

In conclusion, working with an accountant and financial advisor can help safeguard your investment, reduce tax liability, structure deals to minimize risk, and maximize returns. Conduct thorough research, verify credentials and past experience, seek recommendations, interview professionals, understand their fees to find the right accountant and financial advisor for your investment.

Utilizing Property Managers for Real Estate Investment:

Property managers can be valuable assets when it comes to efficiently managing your real estate investments. They can handle various responsibilities such as tenant screening, rent collection, property maintenance, and lease management. Here's when and why you might consider using a property manager:

1. Time and Convenience: If you have limited time or don't want to be involved in the day-to-day operations of managing rental properties, a property manager can handle the tasks for you. This allows you to focus on other aspects of your life or focus on expanding your real estate portfolio.

2. Expertise and Knowledge: Property managers bring experience and expertise in managing properties. They are well-versed in tenant laws, lease agreements, rent collection, property maintenance, and dealing with tenant issues. Their knowledge can help ensure legal compliance and smooth operation of your investments.

3. Tenant Management: Property managers handle tenant screening and selection processes, ensuring that you attract reliable and responsible tenants. They can also manage tenant inquiries, requests, and complaints, saving you time and effort.

4. Maintenance and Repairs: Property managers coordinate property maintenance and address repair needs. They have established

relationships with contractors and can oversee repairs, maintenance, and renovations, ensuring your properties are well-maintained.

Evaluating Property Management Companies:

When selecting a property management company, it's important to carefully evaluate your options to ensure a good fit. Here are some tips for evaluating property management companies:

1. Reputation and Experience: Research the reputation and experience of the property management company. Look for online reviews, testimonials, and ask for references. A well-established company with a positive track record is more likely to provide quality services.

2. Services and Expertise: Consider the range of services offered by the property management company. Ensure they cover your needs, such as tenant screening, rent collection, property maintenance, and lease management. Also, verify their experience managing properties similar to yours.

3. Communication and Responsiveness: Effective communication is crucial when working with a property management company. Assess their response time, availability, and communication channels. Clear and proactive communication helps ensure a smooth working relationship.

4. Fees and Contracts: Understand the fees charged by the property management company and the terms of their contract. Inquire about the management fees, any additional charges, and the length of the contract. Compare these with other companies to ensure competitive pricing.

5. Licensing and Credentials: Check if the property management company is properly licensed and accredited in your jurisdiction. Look

for professional affiliations and certifications indicating their commitment to industry standards and best practices.

6. Personal Meeting: Consider meeting with representatives from the property management company to discuss your needs, ask questions, and assess their professionalism and compatibility.

In conclusion, utilizing a property manager can provide convenience, expertise, and efficient management of real estate investments. Evaluate property management companies based on their reputation, experience, services, communication, fees, licensing, and personal meetings to find the right fit for your needs.

Networking with Other Wholesalers and Investors for Real Estate Investment:

Networking with other wholesalers and investors presents significant benefits in real estate investment. It can lead to joint ventures, shared expertise, ideas, knowledge, and resources to find, negotiate, and close real estate deals. Here are some benefits of forming alliances within the wholesaling community:

1. Shared Opportunities: Networking with other wholesalers and investors exposes you to opportunities you may not have found on your own. By working collaboratively, you can share leads, strategies, and capital, allowing you to expand and grow your real estate portfolio.

2. Shared Expertise: Networking allows you to tap into the knowledge, experience, and expertise of other wholesalers and investors. By working with others, you can learn from their experiences, discover new strategies, and develop your skills to become a more successful investor.

3. Joint Venture Partnerships: Collaborating with other wholesalers and investors can lead to joint venture partnerships. These ventures can allow you to pool resources, expertise, and capital to undertake larger deals, which may not have been possible individually.

4. Increased Accountability: Networking with other wholesalers and investors encourages accountability, which can motivate you to achieve higher levels of success. Collaborating with others can also provide a support system while holding each other accountable, driving growth and increased success.

Strategies for Collaborative Ventures and Shared Opportunities:

Here are some strategies for building alliances and shared opportunities with other wholesalers and investors:

1. Attend Networking Events: Networking events such as meetups, conferences, and real estate clubs can provide an excellent platform to meet other wholesalers and investors. These events provide opportunities to share ideas and knowledge, form partnerships, and find potential joint venture partners.

2. Join Online Groups: Online platforms such as LinkedIn and Facebook groups provide an excellent opportunity to connect with other wholesalers and investors. Joining these groups can provide a wealth of resources, insights, and connections with professionals in the industry.

3. Exchange Referrals: Referral exchange programs with other wholesalers and investors can help expand your potential clients and investors pool. Referring leads to others can lead to more collaborations and deals for you.

4. Collaborate with Complementary Experts: Partnering with complementary experts such as realtors, appraisers, and contractors

can provide value to your joint venture. Collaborating with an expert adds value to the deal and can help you streamline the process.

5. Host Joint Venture Meetings: Hosting joint venture meetings allows you to discuss possible shared opportunities and ventures with other wholesalers and investors. This can lead to new deals, market insights, and continuous learning opportunities.

In conclusion, networking with other wholesalers and real estate investors provides numerous benefits, including shared opportunities, expertise, accountability, and joint venture partnerships. To form alliances, attend networking events, join online groups, exchange referrals, collaborate with complementary experts and host joint venture meetings with others to take advantage of collaborative opportunities.

Certainly! Here's a guide on maintaining professional relationships, including best practices for sustaining long-term relationships and the key elements of communication, trust, and mutual respect.

Maintaining Professional Relationships:

Sustaining professional relationships is critical to your success in any industry. Creating and maintaining strong relationships with colleagues, clients, and other stakeholders helps establish your reputation, network, and opportunities for long-term success. Here are some best practices for maintaining professional relationships:

1. Consistent Communication: Communicating consistently with your colleagues, clients, and stakeholders is crucial. Regular communication builds trust, ensures accountability and alignment, and promotes transparency.

2. Follow-Up and Follow-Through: Following up and following-through on commitments is critical to maintaining professional relationships. Uphold your promises, deliver results, and meet deadlines. Doing what you say builds trust and credibility.

3. Be Responsive: Responding promptly to emails, phone calls, and other requests shows that you value the relationship. It demonstrates your professionalism and accountability. Being unresponsive or delaying a response can harm your reputation and relationships.

4. Show Gratitude: Showing appreciation for your colleagues, clients, and partners helps build stronger relationships. Thanking them for their contributions and acknowledging their efforts and support demonstrates that you recognize their value to you and the business.

5. Be Respectful and Empathetic: Treating people with respect and empathy is crucial to maintaining healthy professional relationships. It involves actively listening, demonstrating understanding, and considering others' opinions and emotions.

Communication, Trust, and Mutual Respect as Key Elements:

Communication, trust, and mutual respect are essential elements of maintaining professional relationships. Effective communication entails active listening, clear and concise messaging, and being open and approachable. Communication allows you to build trust and a deeper understanding of your colleagues, clients, and partners, and helps develop opportunities for collaboration and growth.

Trust is a fundamental building block of any successful relationship. Maintaining trust involves following through with commitments, being transparent, and communicating effectively. Building trust provides a solid foundation for long-term relationships that benefit all parties involved.

Mutual respect involves treating others how you want to be treated. Respecting the opinions, values, and beliefs of your colleagues, clients, and partners opens the door to new opportunities and challenges, enhancing personal and professional growth.

In conclusion, sustaining professional relationships requires dedication, commitment, and a willingness to communicate effectively, build trust, and foster mutual respect. Employing effective communication, following up and following-through, being responsive and showing gratitude are all strategies for maintaining healthy relationships. Communication, trust, and mutual respect are crucial building blocks of any thriving relationship.

Absolutely! Here's a conclusion that summarizes the significance of professional collaborations in real estate wholesaling and encourages the active pursuit and cultivation of relationships with key industry professionals.

Conclusion:

Professional collaborations in real estate wholesaling hold tremendous significance and offer numerous benefits to individuals and businesses in the industry. By actively seeking and cultivating relationships with key industry professionals, wholesalers can unlock a world of opportunities and accelerate their success. Here's a recap of the significance of professional collaborations in real estate wholesaling:

1. Access to Opportunities: Building relationships with other wholesalers, investors, and industry experts provides access to a wide range of opportunities that may not be available otherwise. Through collaborations, wholesalers can discover new leads, gain insights into potential markets, and tap into shared resources and networks.

2. Knowledge Sharing and Skill Development: Collaborating with others allows wholesalers to share knowledge, experiences, and best practices. By learning from one another, wholesalers can enhance their skills, expand their expertise, and stay updated on industry trends. Collaborations foster a culture of continuous learning and improvement.

3. Increased Market Reach: Forming alliances within the wholesaling community expands your market reach. By partnering or networking with other professionals, wholesalers can tap into new markets, leverage their combined resources, and access a broader audience base. This can lead to more successful transactions and greater profitability.

4. Joint Ventures and Shared Ventures: Collaborations often give rise to joint ventures and shared ventures, where wholesalers pool their resources, expertise, and capital to undertake more significant deals. Joint ventures allow wholesalers to take on larger projects and share risks, resulting in enhanced profitability and accelerated growth.

5. Strengthened Reputation and Credibility: Working in collaboration with key industry professionals can significantly enhance a wholesaler's reputation and credibility. By associating with reputable partners and industry experts, wholesalers gain credibility and build trust among potential clients, investors, and other stakeholders.

With these benefits in mind, it is highly encouraged for wholesalers to actively seek and cultivate relationships with key industry professionals. Attend networking events, participate in online communities, and engage in meaningful conversations with fellow wholesalers and investors. Nurture these relationships through regular communication, trust-building efforts, and mutual support.

Remember, professional collaborations are not only about immediate gains but also about long-term growth and success. By fostering strong relationships and partnerships, wholesalers can create a network of trusted professionals who can support and accelerate their journey in real estate wholesaling.

In conclusion, the significance of professional collaborations in real estate wholesaling cannot be overstated. Actively pursuing and cultivating relationships with key industry professionals opens doors to new opportunities, fosters knowledge sharing, expands market reach, and strengthens credibility. Embrace the power of collaboration and watch your wholesaling endeavors thrive.

Part V: The Art of the Deal

Real estate wholesaling, at its core, revolves around the mastery of one critical element: the deal. Navigating this crucial aspect requires more than just understanding market trends and property values; it involves a deep comprehension of negotiation tactics, strategic financing, and the psychology of buying and selling. This part of the book, "The Art of the Deal," is dedicated to unraveling the complexities of creating and closing deals that not only profit but also build a foundation for a sustainable business.

Here, we will explore the intricate dance between buyer and seller, the nuanced art of negotiation, and the strategic decisions that determine the trajectory of a successful wholesale transaction. Each chapter is crafted to equip you with the tools and techniques necessary to thrive in the competitive landscape of real estate wholesaling. From the initial property analysis to the final handshake, understanding the art of the deal is about seeing beyond the immediate transaction to foster relationships, anticipate market shifts, and leverage opportunities for growth.

As we delve into the specifics of deal-making, remember that the most successful wholesalers are not just deal-makers; they are visionary entrepreneurs who treat every deal as a stepping stone towards greater achievements. Whether you are a seasoned wholesaler or new to the industry, mastering the art of the deal is an essential skill that will define your success and longevity in the world of real estate.

Prepare to transform your approach to real estate wholesaling as we uncover the secrets behind crafting deals that are both lucrative and forward-looking, ensuring your position as a leader in the marketplace.

Chapter 9: Finding and Acquiring Properties

In the exciting world of real estate wholesaling, sourcing the right properties is crucial for success. In this chapter, we will explore the importance of finding the right properties and the impact it has on profitability in the wholesaling business.

Overview of the Importance of Sourcing the Right Properties in Wholesaling:

Wholesaling, a popular real estate investment strategy, involves finding properties at a discounted price and then assigning or selling the contract to another buyer for a profit. The success of a wholesaling venture heavily relies on sourcing the right properties.

Sourcing the right properties means identifying properties that are highly marketable, in-demand, and have the potential for a significant profit margin. These properties should meet the criteria of being below market value, allowing room for wholesale investors to purchase them at a discounted price and still sell them at a profit.

By sourcing the right properties, wholesalers can ensure a steady flow of lucrative deals, attracting both buyers and investors. This can lead to multiple opportunities for successful transactions and increased profitability.

Impact of Property Acquisition on Profitability:

Property acquisition plays a vital role in determining the profitability of a wholesaling business. The price at which a wholesaler acquires a property directly affects the potential profit margin.

Acquiring properties at a significant discount provides wholesalers with the opportunity to sell the contracts at a higher price, allowing for a desirable profit margin. Properties purchased at below market value can attract more buyers, creating a competitive market that drives up the wholesale price.

On the other hand, acquiring properties at or above market value can result in a limited profit margin or even financial losses. It is crucial for wholesalers to conduct thorough market research, negotiate effectively, and identify motivated sellers to secure properties at the right price.

Successful property acquisition is not only about the purchase price but also entails assessing the repair costs, market demand, and potential after-repair value (ARV). By intelligently acquiring properties that have the potential to be renovated and sold at a higher value, wholesalers can maximize their profits.

In conclusion, sourcing the right properties and making strategic property acquisitions are essential pillars of success in the wholesaling business. Wholesalers must prioritize finding properties below market value, conducting thorough market research, and understanding the potential profitability of each deal. By doing so, they can position themselves for increased profitability and long-term success in the real estate wholesaling industry.

Understanding Market Dynamics:

To effectively find and acquire profitable properties, it is essential to analyze real estate markets comprehensively. Here are some key steps to understanding market dynamics:

1. Market Research:
Begin by conducting thorough market research to gather data and insights about the local real estate market. Look into factors such as supply and

demand, average property prices, rental rates, vacancy rates, and market trends. This analysis will help you gauge the overall health and potential of the market.

2. Local Economic Factors:
Pay attention to the local economic factors that can impact the real estate market. Look for indicators such as job growth, population trends, infrastructure development, and economic stability. A growing economy can indicate areas with high growth potential and provide opportunities for profitable property acquisitions.

3. Comparative Market Analysis (CMA):
Perform a Comparative Market Analysis (CMA) to evaluate the prices of similar properties in the area. This analysis helps you determine the market value of a property and identify potential deals where properties are priced below market value. Look for motivated sellers, distressed properties, or situations where sellers are willing to negotiate on price.

Identifying Emerging Trends and Areas with High Growth Potential:

To stay ahead in the real estate market, it is crucial to identify emerging trends and areas with high growth potential. Here are some strategies to help you in this endeavor:

1. Market Observation:
Keep an eye on market trends and observe shifts in demand and preferences. Look for areas experiencing revitalization, urban development, or government initiatives. These can be indications of emerging hotspots with high growth potential.

2. Networking:
Build a network of professionals including real estate agents, investors, developers, and industry experts. Attend networking events, join real estate associations, and leverage online platforms to connect with like-minded

individuals. Networking can provide valuable insights about emerging trends and hot markets.

3. Local Knowledge:
Develop a deep understanding of the local area you are targeting. Stay updated on urban planning, zoning regulations, transportation projects, and upcoming developments. This knowledge can uncover opportunities in areas undergoing transformation and experiencing increasing demand.

4. Data Analysis and Technology:
Utilize data analysis tools and technology platforms to identify emerging trends. These tools can help you analyze historical data, spot patterns, and predict future growth in specific neighborhoods or regions. Leverage online platforms, social media, and real estate websites to gather information and track market dynamics.

By effectively analyzing real estate markets and identifying emerging trends and areas with high growth potential, you can position yourself for successful property acquisitions. Understanding market dynamics enables you to find deals with favorable profit margins and capitalize on lucrative opportunities in the ever-evolving real estate industry.

Sourcing Methods:
Finding the right properties for wholesaling requires employing effective sourcing methods. In this chapter, we will discuss various approaches to sourcing properties, including direct mail campaigns, online platforms and MLS, driving for dollars, and collaborating with wholesalers and bird dogs. Let's explore these methods in a simpler and more understandable manner.

1. Direct Mail Campaigns: Strategy and Execution:

Direct mail campaigns involve sending targeted mailers to potential sellers in specific areas. Here's a simplified breakdown of the strategy and execution:

- Identify Target Area: Focus on areas with high potential for distressed or motivated sellers. Conduct market research and identify neighborhoods with desirable properties.

- Build a Mailing List: Compile a list of addresses within your target area using resources like public records, specialized software, or purchasing lists from reputable vendors.

- Craft Persuasive Mailers: Design compelling and personalized mailers that grab the attention of potential sellers. Highlight the benefits of a quick and hassle-free sale, emphasizing your expertise as a wholesaler.

- Execute the Campaign: Send out the mailers consistently and monitor the response rate. Follow up with interested sellers and negotiate favorable deals.

2. Online Platforms and MLS: Leveraging Technology to Find Deals:

Online platforms and Multiple Listing Services (MLS) provide access to a wide range of property listings. Here's a simplified approach:
MmResearch Online Platforms: Explore real estate websites, online marketplaces, and MLS platforms. Use filters to narrow down your search based on location, price range, property type, and other relevant criteria.

- Analyze Listings: Evaluate each listing, considering factors like price, condition, market demand, and potential profit margin. Pay attention to motivated sellers or distressed properties that offer room for negotiation.

- Leverage Technology Tools: Utilize data analysis tools, AI-based algorithms, and virtual tours to make informed decisions and identify potential deals.

3. Driving for Dollars: On-the-Ground Tactics for Uncovering Opportunities:

Driving for dollars involves physically exploring target neighborhoods to discover distressed or vacant properties. Simplified steps include:

- Choose a Target Area: Select neighborhoods with potential for distressed or motivated sellers. Look for signs of neglect, vacant properties, or properties in need of repair.

- Drive and Document: Drive through the chosen area, documenting any properties that appear vacant, overgrown, or showing signs of distress. Take note of addresses and other relevant details.

- Research and Follow Up: Research the ownership and contact information of the identified properties. Reach out to the owners, expressing your interest in purchasing the property and offering a quick and hassle-free transaction.

4. Working with Wholesalers and Bird Dogs:

Collaborating with wholesalers and bird dogs can expand your sourcing network and increase the chances of finding lucrative deals. Simplified steps include:

- Connect and Build Relationships: Network with experienced wholesalers and bird dogs through real estate events, online platforms, or local associations. Establish mutually beneficial relationships based on trust and professionalism.

- Communicate Your Criteria: Clearly communicate the types of properties and deals you are interested in. Provide specific details like price range, location, and desired profit margin.

- Incentivize Referrals: Offer competitive referral fees or commissions to wholesalers or bird dogs who bring you successful leads or deals.

By simplifying the concepts and steps involved in these sourcing methods, we aim to make it easier for individuals to understand and implement them in their journey of finding properties for wholesaling. Each method has its own advantages, and it's important to explore and experiment with different approaches to identify what works best for you.

Evaluating properties:

Evaluating properties is a critical step in the real estate investment process. In this chapter, we will discuss three methods for property evaluation: conducting initial assessments remotely, physical inspections, and utilizing financial models for deal viability. Let's explore these methods in detail.

1. Conducting Initial Property Assessments Remotely:

When evaluating properties remotely, here are some key factors to consider:

- Property Information: Gather as much information as possible about the property, including details on size, layout, condition, age, amenities, and any recent renovations.

- Photos and Videos: Request comprehensive photos or videos of the property, both interior and exterior. Look for signs of structural issues, maintenance needs, or potential value-added opportunities.

- Online Research: Utilize online resources to gather data about the neighborhood, recent sales prices, rental rates, and market trends. This information will help you assess the property's potential return on investment.

- Virtual Tours: Where available, take advantage of virtual tours or 3D walkthroughs to gain a better understanding of the property's layout and condition.

Remember, while remote assessments provide a preliminary evaluation, conducting physical inspections is crucial for a comprehensive property evaluation.

2. Physical Inspections and What to Look For:

When conducting physical inspections, carefully assess the property using the following guidelines:

- Structural Integrity: Inspect the foundation, walls, roof, and overall structural condition. Look for signs of cracks, water damage, sagging structures, or other red flags that may require costly repairs.

- Plumbing and Electrical Systems: Check for leaks, water pressure issues, faulty wiring, or outdated electrical panels. Inadequate plumbing or electrical systems can significantly affect the property's value and increase future expenses.

- Interior Condition: Evaluate the condition of floors, walls, cabinets, appliances, and fixtures. Consider the cost and effort required to renovate or update these elements.

- Exterior Features: Assess the yard, landscaping, parking space, and any outdoor amenities. These aspects can influence a property's appeal and potential rental or resale value.

- Safety and Compliance: Ensure the property meets safety standards and complies with local building codes. Evaluate issues such as proper ventilation, fire safety measures, and accessibility features.

Remember to hire a professional inspector for a detailed assessment, particularly for complex properties or if you lack expertise in construction and building systems.

3. Using Financial Models to Evaluate Deal Viability:

Financial models help determine the profitability and viability of a real estate investment. Consider the following factors:

- Cash Flow Analysis: Calculate the potential rental income and compare it with expenses such as mortgage payments, property taxes, insurance, maintenance costs, and vacancy rates. A positive cash flow indicates a potentially profitable investment.

- Return on Investment (ROI): Determine the projected return on investment by considering the purchase price, renovation costs, and estimated future value. This analysis assists in evaluating the profitability of the investment over time.

- Cap Rate and Cash-on-Cash Return: Calculate the property's capitalization rate (Cap Rate) and cash-on-cash return to assess its income potential and compare it to other investment options.

- Sensitivity Analysis: Conduct sensitivity analysis by modeling different scenarios, such as changes in rental income, interest rates, or market conditions. This analysis helps identify potential risks and adjust investment strategies accordingly.

Consider using software or financial tools specifically designed for real estate investment analysis to streamline the process and obtain accurate results.

By employing these evaluation methods, you can make informed decisions about the viability and profitability of potential real estate deals. Balancing remote assessments, physical inspections, and financial modeling allows you to evaluate properties comprehensively and mitigate potential risks.

Negotiating Deals

Negotiating deals is a crucial skill in real estate wholesaling. In this chapter, we will discuss the basic principles of negotiation tailored to real estate wholesaling, common negotiation strategies, and how to apply them in different scenarios. We will also explore overcoming common challenges and obstacles in deal negotiation. Let's dive in!

1. Basic Principles of Negotiation Tailored to Real Estate Wholesaling:

When negotiating deals in real estate wholesaling, keep these principles in mind:

- Preparation: Thoroughly research the property, market conditions, and the seller's motivations and needs. This knowledge empowers you to negotiate from an informed position.

- Active Listening: Listen actively to the seller's concerns, preferences, and priorities. Understanding their perspective allows you to craft win-win solutions.

- Clear Communication: Clearly articulate your objectives, concerns, and proposed terms. Transparency and effective communication build trust and facilitate a productive negotiation process.

- Flexibility: Be open to creative solutions and flexible in exploring alternative options that can benefit both parties. This can help overcome impasses and find mutually agreeable terms.

- Patience: Negotiations can take time. Be patient and persistent, understanding that finding common ground may require multiple rounds of discussion and negotiation.

2. Common Negotiation Strategies and How to Apply Them in Different Scenarios:

Here are some common negotiation strategies used in real estate wholesaling:

- Win-Win Approach: Strive for a win-win outcome where both parties feel satisfied with the deal. Look for ways to meet the seller's needs while achieving your own goals.

- Building Rapport: Cultivate a positive and mutually respectful relationship with the seller. Establishing rapport can lead to smoother negotiations and greater cooperation.

- Anchoring: Begin the negotiation with a strong initial offer that serves as an anchor point for further discussions. This can influence the perception of value and potentially lead to favorable terms.

- Offering Multiple Options: Present the seller with multiple offers or deal structures. This provides them with choice and increases the likelihood of finding a mutually acceptable agreement.

- Use of Time: Utilize time as a negotiating tool. Deadlines and time-sensitive offers can create a sense of urgency and encourage the seller to make a decision.

- Creative Problem Solving: Think outside the box and explore creative solutions that address the concerns and priorities of both parties. This can lead to unique and mutually beneficial agreements.

3. Overcoming Common Challenges and Obstacles in Deal Negotiation:

Deal negotiation can present challenges. Here are strategies for overcoming common obstacles:

- Objection Handling: Anticipate and address objections by thoroughly understanding the seller's concerns. Prepare persuasive counterarguments that highlight the benefits of your offer.

- Overcoming Price Resistance: If the seller is resistant to the proposed price, focus on other aspects that may add value, such as quick and hassle-free transactions, flexibility in closing dates, or addressing other specific needs they may have.

- Building Trust: Establish and maintain trust throughout the negotiation process. Be honest, transparent, and reliable in your interactions. Building trust can help navigate challenging or contentious discussions.

- Negotiating Repairs: If repairs are needed, negotiate fair terms based on accurate assessments of the property condition. Consider sharing repair cost estimates or offering credits to address the concerns.

Remember, negotiation requires adaptability, perseverance, and the ability to find common ground. By applying these strategies and overcoming challenges, you can successfully negotiate favorable deals in real estate wholesaling.

Negotiating deals in real estate wholesaling involves understanding fundamental principles, employing effective strategies, and navigating challenges. By preparing thoroughly, listening actively, and communicating clearly, you can build rapport, explore creative solutions, and achieve mutually beneficial agreements. Keep practicing and refining your negotiation skills to become a successful real estate wholesaler.

Financing Options for Acquisition

When acquiring properties, it is essential to consider the various financing methods available. In this chapter, we will provide an overview of financing options suitable for acquisition and discuss the pros and cons of each method, including cash, loans, and partnerships. Let's explore these financing options in more detail.

1. Cash:

Using cash to finance acquisitions involves paying the full purchase price upfront without the need for external financing. Here are some pros and cons of using cash for acquisitions:

Pros:
- Quick and Simple: With cash, there is no need to go through the loan approval process, allowing for a faster transaction.
- Negotiation Power: Cash offers may be more appealing to sellers, giving you an advantage in negotiations and potentially securing better purchase terms.
- No Interest Payments: By using cash, you can avoid interest payments associated with loans, which can save you money in the long run.

Cons:
- Liquidation of Assets: Using cash may require liquidating other assets or depleting cash reserves, which can limit investment opportunities or leave you with reduced financial flexibility.
- Opportunity Cost: Deploying a large amount of cash for a property acquisition means potentially missing out on other investment opportunities.
- Lack of Leverage: Cash purchases do not offer leverage advantages, such as using borrowed funds to amplify returns.

2. Loans:

Real estate loans provide financing options for property acquisitions. Here are the pros and cons of using loans:

Pros:
- Leverage: Loans allow you to leverage funds, enabling you to acquire properties with a smaller initial investment while potentially maximizing your return on investment. Preserve Cash Reserves: By utilizing loans, you can preserve your cash reserves for other investment opportunities or emergencies.
- Tax Benefits: Mortgage interest and other loan-related expenses may be tax-deductible, offering potential tax benefits.

Cons:
- Interest Payments: Loans come with interest payments, which increase the overall cost of acquiring the property.
- Qualification Requirements: Loan approval depends on factors such as creditworthiness, income, and the property's appraisal value, which can be challenging to meet for some investors.
- Debt Obligation: Loans create a long-term debt obligation that needs to be repaid, which can impact cash flow and financial flexibility.

3. Partnerships:

Another option for financing property acquisitions is partnering with other investors. Here are the pros and cons of partnerships:

Pros:
- Shared Risk: Partnering with others can help distribute the financial risk associated with property acquisitions.

- Pooling Resources: Partnerships allow investors to combine their financial resources, increasing their purchasing power and the potential for larger and more profitable acquisitions.
- Access to Expertise: Partnerships often bring together individuals with different skills and knowledge, providing access to diverse expertise in real estate investing.

Cons:
- Shared Decision-Making: In partnerships, decisions need to be made collectively, which may result in conflicts or delays in the decision-making process.
- Profit Sharing: Partnerships involve sharing profits and potentially giving up a portion of the investment return.
- Alignment of Goals and Vision: Partnerships require clear communication and alignment of goals, long-term strategies, and the vision for the property.

Choosing the right financing option for property acquisitions involves weighing the pros and cons of each method. Cash offers simplicity and negotiation power but may limit financial flexibility. Loans provide leverage and preserve cash reserves, but come with interest payments and qualification requirements. Partnerships allow shared risk and pooled resources, but necessitate shared decision-making and profit sharing. Evaluating your financial situation, investment goals, and risk tolerance will help guide you in selecting the most suitable financing option for your property acquisitions.

The Role of Due Diligence

Due diligence is a crucial process in real estate acquisitions, involving a comprehensive assessment of various aspects of the property. In this chapter, we will explore the role of due diligence and discuss its three key components: legal due diligence, physical due diligence, and financial due diligence. Let's delve into each of these areas in more detail.

1. Legal Due Diligence:

Legal due diligence focuses on examining the legal aspects of the property. Here are some key areas of legal due diligence:

- Titles: Confirming the ownership of the property by reviewing title documents and ensuring there are no disputes or claims on the title that could affect the acquisition.

- Liens and Encumbrances: Investigating any liens, mortgages, or other encumbrances on the property to ensure a clear title transfer. This may involve reviewing public records, tax records, and survey reports.

- Contracts and Legal Obligations: Reviewing existing contracts, leases, and legal obligations associated with the property, such as easements or restrictive covenants.

Legal due diligence helps identify potential legal risks or issues that could impact the acquisition or affect future ownership and operation of the property.

2. Physical Due Diligence:

Physical due diligence involves assessing the condition and suitability of the property. Here are some key areas of physical due diligence:

- Inspections: Conducting thorough property inspections, including structural, mechanical, electrical, and environmental inspections, to identify any existing or potential issues that may require repairs or remediation.

- Appraisals: Evaluating the property's market value through an appraisal to ensure it aligns with the purchase price and to determine its potential for appreciation.
- Assessments: Reviewing any existing assessments or studies related to the property, such as environmental assessments, zoning compliance, or land use evaluations.

Physical due diligence helps assess the property's physical condition, identify potential risks or issues, and estimate any necessary repairs or improvements.

3. Financial Due Diligence:

Financial due diligence involves verifying the financial aspects of the property acquisition. Here are some key areas of financial due diligence:

- Costs and Expenses: Reviewing past and projected costs associated with the property, such as taxes, insurance, maintenance, and utilities, to ensure they align with the intended investment strategy.

- Anticipated Revenues: Evaluating the property's income potential, such as rental income or revenue from commercial operations, to assess its financial viability and potential return on investment.

Financial due diligence helps validate the financial feasibility of the property acquisition and provides insights into the expected costs, revenues, and potential profitability.

Due diligence plays a vital role in real estate acquisitions, providing a comprehensive assessment of the property's legal, physical, and financial aspects. Legal due diligence ensures a clear title, identifies potential legal issues, and verifies legal obligations. Physical due diligence helps assess the property's condition, uncovering any structural, environmental, or other physical concerns. Financial due diligence validates the financial aspects of the acquisition, including costs, revenues, and potential profitability. Conducting thorough due diligence helps mitigate risks, make informed decisions, and maximize the chances of a successful property acquisition.

Closing the Deal

Closing the deal is the final step in a real estate transaction, where ownership is transferred from the seller to the buyer. In this chapter, we will discuss the steps to ensure a smooth closing process, common closing hurdles, and strategies to overcome them. Let's explore these aspects of closing in more detail.

1. Ensuring a Smooth Closing Process:

To ensure a smooth closing process, consider the following steps:

- Preparing Closing Documents: Work with your attorney or closing agent to prepare all necessary documents, including the purchase agreement, deed, title transfer documents, and any required disclosures.

- Clearing Contingencies: Review and fulfill any contingencies specified in the purchase agreement, such as satisfactory property inspections, obtaining financing, or resolving any outstanding legal or Title issues.

- Scheduling the Closing: Coordinate with all parties involved, including the buyer, seller, real estate agents, attorneys, and lenders, to set a mutually convenient date, time, and location for the closing.

- Conducting a Final Walk-through: Prior to the closing, schedule a final walk-through of the property to ensure it is in the agreed-upon condition and any requested repairs have been completed.

- Securing Funds: Arrange for the necessary funds for the closing, including down payment, closing costs, and any additional fees or escrow accounts required.

By following these steps, you can help facilitate a smooth and efficient closing process.

2. Overcoming Common Closing Hurdles:

During the closing process, various hurdles may arise. Here are some common hurdles and strategies to overcome them:

- Financing Issues: If there are delays or issues with securing financing, work closely with your lender to address any concerns, provide requested documentation promptly, and explore alternative solutions if necessary.

- Title or Legal Concerns: If title issues, liens, or legal complications arise, involve your attorney to help resolve the problems and ensure a clear title transfer.

- Appraisal or Inspection Discrepancies: If there are discrepancies in the appraisal value or inspection reports, negotiate with the seller to reach an agreement on necessary repairs, price adjustments, or escrow accounts to cover potential issues.

- Delays in Document Processing: If there are delays in document processing or review, maintain regular communication with all parties involved, follow up with any requested information promptly, and consider setting realistic timelines for the closing.

By staying proactive, maintaining open lines of communication, and working closely with the professionals involved, you can overcome many common closing hurdles.

3. Finalizing Transactions and Transferring Ownership:

During the closing, the following activities take place:

- Reviewing and Signing Documents: Review and sign all necessary closing documents, including the deed, mortgage or loan documents, title transfer forms, and any other required paperwork.

- Payment and Fund Disbursement: Provide the necessary funds for the closing, which typically include the down payment, closing costs, and any other agreed-upon payments. The funds are then disbursed to the appropriate parties, such as the seller, real estate agents, and service providers.

- Transfer of Ownership: Once all documents are signed, funds are disbursed, and legal requirements are met, the ownership of the property is officially transferred from the seller to the buyer.

Closing the deal requires careful preparation, effective communication, and attention to detail. By following the steps to ensure a smooth closing process, being proactive in addressing common closing hurdles, and finalizing the transaction by signing all necessary documents and transferring ownership, you can successfully complete the real estate acquisition process.

Building a Pipeline

Building a pipeline of property prospects is essential for successful real estate acquisitions, ensuring a consistent flow of opportunities and a higher probability of finding desirable properties. In this chapter, we will explore strategies for maintaining a consistent flow of property prospects and scaling property acquisition efforts effectively.

1. Strategies for a Consistent Flow of Property Prospects:

To maintain a consistent flow of property prospects, consider the following strategies:

- Networking: Build relationships with real estate agents, brokers, and other industry professionals to tap into their network of potential sellers and off-market properties.

- Marketing: Invest in effective marketing strategies, such as targeted direct mail campaigns, online ads, and social media promotion to raise awareness of your business and attract potential sellers.

- Referrals: Request referrals from satisfied clients, business partners, and industry professionals to expand your network of potential sellers and create word-of-mouth advertising.

- Research: Conduct in-depth market research to identify trends, hotspots, and opportunities in key markets and niches, and use this data to locate potential properties and sellers.

By adopting these strategies, you can create a consistent flow of property prospects and increase the chances of finding attractive and profitable opportunities.

2. Scaling Property Acquisition Efforts Effectively:

To scale property acquisition efforts effectively, consider the following strategies:

- Automating Processes: Automate key processes, such as lead generation and follow-up, marketing, and document management, to save time and increase efficiency.

- Hiring and Outsourcing: Hire and outsource key roles such as real estate agents, property managers, attorneys, and accountants to leverage their expertise and free up time for other activities.

- Leveraging Technology: Utilize technology tools such as real estate databases, CRM systems, and project management software to streamline workflows, manage teams, and track progress.

- Establishing Partnerships: Collaborate with other investors, developers, or companies to pool resources, share knowledge, and expand the scope of your property acquisition efforts.

By adopting these strategies, you can increase your capacity for property acquisition and achieve economies of scale, resulting in higher profitability and a more robust real estate portfolio.

Building a pipeline of property prospects and scaling property acquisition efforts require a proactive and strategic approach to real estate investing. By leveraging networking, marketing, referrals, and research to maintain a consistent flow of property prospects, and by automating, hiring, outsourcing, leveraging technology, and establishing partnerships to scale property acquisition efforts, you can achieve success and build a substantial and profitable real estate portfolio.

Conclusion

In this comprehensive guide to property acquisition in real estate, we have covered a range of topics, including the importance of due diligence, key metrics for evaluating properties, financing options, conducting negotiations, closing the deal, and building a pipeline of property prospects.

Summary of key takeaways from the chapter:

1. Conduct thorough due diligence to verify property information, assess market trends and conditions, and mitigate risks.

2. Use key metrics, such as cap rate, ROI, cash-on-cash return, and net operating income, to evaluate properties and determine their profitability.

3. Understand and evaluate different financing options, including conventional mortgages, hard money loans, and seller financing, to choose the best fit for your investment strategy.

4. Develop effective negotiation skills to build trust, establish rapport, and achieve win-win outcomes that benefit both parties.

5. Focus on building a pipeline of property prospects by leveraging networking, marketing, referrals, and research strategies.

6. Use automation, outsourcing, technology, and partnerships to increase efficiency, scale your property acquisition efforts, and achieve greater profitability.

Motivational closing that emphasizes the strategic value of proficient property acquisition:

- Proficient property acquisition is not just about investing in real estate; it's about building a legacy that can last for generations. Through careful research, due diligence, and effective negotiation, you can identify profitable properties and create value that can benefit both you and the community. By building a pipeline of property prospects and scaling your efforts, you can amplify your success and build a substantial and profitable real estate portfolio that can provide financial security and peace of mind for years to come.

So, go out and seize the opportunity to acquire properties with confidence, conviction, and competence. With a strategic mindset, diligence, and commitment, you can harness the power of real estate and create a brighter and more prosperous future.

Chapter 10: Mastering Property Valuation

Property valuation plays a crucial role in the realm of real estate wholesaling. It serves as the foundation upon which various aspects of the business are built and executed. In this chapter, we will explore the importance of accurate property valuation and how it impacts every facet of the wholesaling industry. By understanding the dynamics of property valuation, aspiring wholesalers can gain a competitive edge and improve their chances of success.

Importance of Accurate Property Valuation in Real Estate Wholesaling: Accurate property valuation is the cornerstone of real estate wholesaling. It refers to the process of establishing the true market value of a property based on various factors such as location, condition, size, and comparable sales. A precise valuation is essential for wholesalers as it directly affects their ability to secure profitable deals and maximize their potential earnings. Here's why accurate property valuation is crucial:

1. Identifying Attractive Investment Opportunities: By assessing the market value of a property accurately, wholesalers can spot lucrative investment opportunities. This enables them to identify distressed properties, motivated sellers, and undervalued assets that hold great potential for profit. Accurate valuation acts as a compass, guiding wholesalers toward the right deals and helping them make informed investment decisions.

2. Negotiating with Confidence: When wholesalers possess a deep understanding of property valuation, they can negotiate deals with confidence. Being able to provide an accurate assessment of a property's worth empowers wholesalers to present compelling offers

to sellers. This not only increases the chances of striking a mutually beneficial deal but also strengthens the wholesaler's credibility and reputation within the industry.

3. Determining Wholesale Prices: The wholesaling business is based on the principle of buying properties at a discounted price and selling them to investors or end buyers for a profit. Accurate property valuation enables wholesalers to determine the optimal wholesale price for a property. By considering the property's market value, repair costs, and potential resale value, wholesalers can set prices that attract potential buyers while ensuring a satisfactory profit margin for themselves.

Impact of Valuation on Every Aspect of the Wholesaling Business: Property valuation significantly influences various facets of the real estate wholesaling business. Let's explore how it impacts each of these areas:

1. Lead Generation: Accurate property valuation helps wholesalers filter and prioritize leads effectively. Having a clear understanding of market values allows them to focus on properties with the highest potential for profitability, saving time and effort.

2. Marketing and Advertising: When wholesalers accurately assess a property's value, they can craft compelling marketing campaigns that highlight its unique selling points. Effective advertising strategies built on accurate valuation foster interest among potential buyers and increase the likelihood of closing deals successfully.

3. Due Diligence and Analysis: Property valuation forms the foundation for conducting thorough due diligence. Wholesalers need to assess a property's condition, examine its legal and financial aspects, and evaluate the surrounding neighborhood. Accurate valuation ensures comprehensive analysis, mitigating risks and enabling wholesalers to make informed decisions.

4. Negotiation and Deal Structuring: Accurate valuation equips wholesalers with the knowledge to negotiate effectively. By understanding a property's market value, wholesalers can structure deals that align with the specific needs and expectations of buyers and sellers, increasing the odds of a successful transaction.

Mastering property valuation is essential for success in the real estate wholesaling industry. Accurate valuation enables wholesalers to identify attractive opportunities, negotiate confidently, and determine optimal wholesale prices. It impacts every aspect of the wholesaling business, from lead generation to marketing, due diligence, and deal structuring. By gaining a comprehensive understanding of property valuation, aspiring wholesalers can navigate the industry with ease and enhance their chances of achieving profitable outcomes.

Basics of Property Valuation:
Essential Concepts and Methods for Real Estate Wholesaling

In the world of real estate overselling, accurate property valuation is critical. Valuation helps wholesalers determine the true worth of a property and make informed investment decisions. In this chapter, we will discuss the crucial concepts and methods used in property valuation. By understanding the fundamental principles of market value, investment value, and distressed value, and common valuation methods, aspiring wholesalers can gain a competitive edge and improve their chances of success.

Definition of Key Valuation Concepts:
There are three essential concepts that aspiring wholesalers must understand to master property valuation. These concepts are market value, investment value, and distressed value.

1. Market Value: Market value refers to the price at which a property would sell in the current market conditions, assuming no undue

influence or pressure. The market value of a property is determined by the interaction of supply and demand, and factors such as location, size, condition, and comparable sales.

2. Investment Value: Investment value, on the other hand, refers to the specific value of a property to a particular investor based on their individual financial goals. It differs from market value, as it takes into account the investor's specific requirements and motivations.

3. Distressed Value: Distressed value refers to the value of a property in a distressed state, such as foreclosure, abandonment, or disrepair. It is typically lower than the market or investment values and represents an opportunity for wholesalers to acquire properties at a discounted price.

Overview of Common Valuation Methods Used in Real Estate:
Several methods are used in real estate valuation to determine the worth of a property accurately. Here are some common methods:

1. Sales Comparison Method: The sales comparison method is a widely used valuation approach that compares the subject property with recently sold properties in the same location with similar characteristics. This method is used to determine the market value of a property and is based on the principle of substitution, which assumes that buyers will not pay more for a property if they can find a comparable one at a lower price.

2. Income Capitalization Method: The income capitalization method is used to determine the value of a property based on its income-generating potential. It considers the rental income, operating expenses, and capitalization rate to estimate the property's value. This approach is typically used to value commercial properties, rental properties, and other income-generating assets.

3. Cost Approach Method: The cost approach method is a valuation method that estimates the property's value by determining the cost to reproduce or replace it. It considers the value of the land, replacement cost of the building, and depreciation. This approach is typically used to value new or unique properties or properties with significant improvements.

Understanding the key concepts and common methods used in property valuation is essential for aspiring wholesalers. Accurate valuation is the foundation of successful real estate wholesaling, and a comprehensive understanding of market value, investment value, and distressed value can provide a competitive advantage. By mastering the common valuation methods, wholesalers can evaluate properties effectively and make informed investment decisions that lead to profitable outcomes.

Mastering Comparative Market Analysis (CMA) for Real Estate Wholesaling

Competitive Market Analysis (CMA) is a widely used valuation approach in the real estate industry. It's a comparative method to determine a property's market value by analyzing recently sold and similar properties. In this chapter, we will explore the essential steps to conduct a CMA, how to select and analyze comparables, and the adjustments required for differences between properties to arrive at an accurate market value.

Steps to Conduct a CMA:
Conducting a CMA involves several steps that aspiring wholesalers must follow. Here's a breakdown of the process:

1. Define the Subject Property: The first step in conducting a CMA is to identify the subject property. The subject property is the property that you want to determine the market value for. It's essential to have a thorough understanding of the subject property's features, such as location, size, condition, and amenities.

2. Select Comparable Properties: The next step is to select comparable properties, also known as "comparables." Comparables are recently sold properties that are similar to the subject property in terms of location, size, condition, and amenities.

3. Analyze the Comparable Properties: Once you have identified potential comparables, the next step is to analyze them and determine how similar they are to the subject property. Factors to consider include the location, number of bedrooms and bathrooms, square footage, lot size, age, and condition.

4. Adjust for Differences: No two properties are identical, and differences between the subject property and comparables must be accounted for. Common adjustments include size, condition, amenities, and location.

5. Determine the Estimated Market Value: After making the necessary adjustments to the comparable properties, the final step is to determine the estimated market value for the subject property. This value is based on the adjusted sale prices of the comparable properties.

How to Select and Analyze Comparables:
Choosing the right comparables and analyzing them effectively requires a keen understanding of property valuation. Here are some key factors to consider when selecting comparables:

1. Location:Location is one of the most crucial factors when selecting comparables. Ideally, comparables should be located within the same

neighborhood, subdivision, or city. Factors to consider include proximity to schools, shopping centers, and transportation.

2. Size: Comparables should be similar in size to the subject property. Matching square footage and lot size are essential in determining the market value accurately.

3. Condition: The condition of the comparables should be considered when selecting them. Ideally, comparables should be in a similar state of repair to the subject property.

Adjustments for Differences Between Properties:
Adjustments are essential in ensuring that comparables and the subject property are as similar as possible. Factors that require adjustment include:

1. Size: Properties with differing square footage will require size adjustments. Adjustments are made by multiplying the price per square foot by the difference in square footage.

2. Condition: When the condition of the comparables and the subject property vary, condition adjustments are necessary. Home repairs, updates, and renovations are all considered in the adjustment.

3. Amenities: Properties with additional features such as pools, garages, and outdoor kitchens will require adjustments for amenities.

CMA is a valuable tool to determine market values accurately. By understanding the steps involved in conducting a CMA, selecting and analyzing comparables, and making necessary adjustments, wholesalers can conduct accurate and insightful competitive market analyses. A thorough understanding of property valuation and CMA is a crucial skill for any real estate investor looking to achieve success.

Mastering the Income Approach for Property Valuation

The income approach is a commonly used method for valuing real estate properties. It focuses on the property's income-generating potential and is particularly useful for commercial properties and rental properties. In this chapter, we will explore the income approach in detail, including an explanation of the approach, how to calculate Net Operating Income (NOI), and the utilization of capitalization rates to estimate property value.

Explanation of the Income Approach to Valuation:
The income approach to valuation is based on the principle that the value of a property is determined by its income-generating potential. It considers the Net Operating Income (NOI) of the property and applies a capitalization rate to estimate its value. This approach is especially relevant for properties that generate rental income, such as apartment buildings, office complexes, and retail centers.

Calculating Net Operating Income (NOI):
The first step in applying the income approach is to calculate the Net Operating Income (NOI) of the property. NOI is the income generated by the property after deducting operating expenses but before deducting mortgage payments or taxes. The formula to calculate NOI is:

NOI = Potential Rental Income - Vacancy and Collection Losses - Operating Expenses

Potential Rental Income refers to the total rental income the property could generate if all units or spaces were occupied and rented at market rates. Vacancy and Collection Losses account for any potential lost rental income due to vacancies or unpaid rent. Operating Expenses include costs such as property management fees, maintenance expenses, insurance, property taxes, and utilities.

Utilizing Capitalization Rates to Estimate Property Value:
Once the NOI is calculated, the next step is to estimate the property's value using a capitalization rate (cap rate). The capitalization rate represents the rate of return an investor requires on their investment. It is calculated by dividing the NOI by the property's value:

Property Value = NOI / Capitalization Rate

The capitalization rate is determined based on various factors such as the property type, location, market conditions, and the investor's risk tolerance. It can be derived by analyzing similar properties in the market or obtained from industry reports.

The income approach is a valuable method for valuing income-generating properties. By calculating the Net Operating Income (NOI) and utilizing a suitable capitalization rate, investors can estimate the value of a property based on its income potential. The income approach provides critical insights into the investment value of commercial and rental properties and is an essential tool in the real estate valuation toolbox.

Understanding the Cost Approach in Real Estate Wholesaling

The cost approach is one of the three primary methods used to value real estate properties, alongside the income approach and sales comparison approach. It is particularly useful when valuing new or unique properties. In this chapter, we will explore the cost approach in depth, including when to use it, how to calculate replacement cost and depreciation, and the limitations and practical use cases of the cost approach in wholesaling.

When to Use the Cost Approach:
The cost approach is commonly used in the following scenarios:

1. New Construction: When valuing newly constructed properties with limited sales data, the cost approach becomes vital. It provides an estimate of the property's value based on the cost to construct it.

2. Unique or Special Purpose Properties: Properties that possess unique features or serve specific purposes, such as churches, government buildings, or schools, often lack comparable sales data. In such cases, the cost approach helps estimate their value based on the cost to replicate them.

Calculating Replacement Cost and Depreciation:
To apply the cost approach, you need to calculate the replacement cost and account for depreciation. Here's how it's done:

1. Replacement Cost: Replacement cost refers to the cost of constructing an identical or similar property at current market rates. It considers material and labor costs, permits, and other expenses. It is essential to consult with contractors or use reputable cost estimation tools to arrive at an accurate replacement cost figure.

2. Depreciation: Depreciation accounts for the loss of value or obsolescence of a property over time. There are three main types of depreciation:

- Physical Depreciation: This refers to the deterioration of the property itself due to wear and tear, aging, or lack of maintenance. It is estimated by considering factors such as the property's age, condition, and remaining useful life.

- Functional Depreciation: Functional depreciation occurs when a property's design or layout becomes less desirable or outdated compared to newer properties. It accounts for any deficiencies or inefficiencies in the property's structure or features.

- External/Externalities Depreciation: External depreciation considers factors external to the property itself, such as changes in the surrounding neighborhood, zoning regulations, or economic factors. It takes into account how these external factors may have an impact on the property's value.

Limitations and Practical Use Cases of the Cost Approach in Wholesaling: It's important to be aware of the limitations of the cost approach in wholesaling:

1. Difficulty in Estimating Accurate Replacement Cost: Calculating an accurate replacement cost can be challenging, especially when dealing with unique or specialized properties. Construction costs may vary, and market conditions can influence pricing.

2. Subjectivity in Depreciation Estimation: Estimating depreciation requires some subjectivity, particularly when assessing functional or external depreciation. It relies on the expertise and judgment of the appraiser or wholesaler.

Practical use cases of the cost approach in wholesaling include:

1. Estimating Value for New Development Opportunities: When wholesaling potential development sites, the cost approach helps determine the value based on the cost to construct new buildings.

2. Evaluating Unique or Special Purpose Properties: The cost approach is valuable when dealing with properties that lack comparable sales data, such as historical buildings, government facilities, or properties with unique features.

The cost approach is a valuable tool in real estate wholesaling, particularly for new construction and unique properties. By calculating the replacement cost and accounting for depreciation, wholesalers can estimate a property's value. However, it's crucial to be aware of the limitations and exercise caution when applying the cost approach, as accurate estimation of replacement costs can be challenging, and the subjectivity of depreciation estimation adds complexity.

Exploring Automated Valuation Models (AVM) in Real Estate Wholesaling

Technological advancements have revolutionized the field of property valuation, offering efficient and automated solutions. Automated Valuation Models (AVMs) are computer-based tools that use algorithms and data analysis to estimate property values. In this chapter, we will provide an overview of technological tools in property valuation, specifically focusing on AVMs. We will discuss the pros and cons of using AVMs in real estate wholesaling.

Overview of Technological Tools in Property Valuation:
Technological tools have significantly transformed the property valuation process. They leverage vast troves of data, including property characteristics, comparable sales, market trends, and other factors. Some commonly used technological tools include:

1. Automated Valuation Models (AVMs): AVMs employ algorithms to estimate property values based on various data inputs. They provide a quick and automated valuation estimate.

2. Geographic Information Systems (GIS): GIS tools integrate spatial data, such as maps and aerial imagery, with property information to enhance analysis and visualization.

3. Data Analytics and Machine Learning: Advanced data analytics and machine learning algorithms are used to extract insights from vast datasets, identify patterns, and predict property values based on historical data.

Pros of Using AVMs in Real Estate Wholesaling:
1. Efficiency and Speed: AVMs offer fast valuation estimates, allowing wholesalers to evaluate numerous properties quickly. This saves time and resources.

2. Cost-Effectiveness: AVMs can provide valuation estimates at a fraction of the cost of traditional appraisals, making them a cost-effective option for wholesalers.

3. Accessibility to Data: AVMs leverage vast databases and can access comprehensive property data, market trends, and historical sales information, providing wholesalers with a wealth of information.

Cons of Using AVMs in Real Estate Wholesaling:
1. Lack of Human Judgment: AVMs rely solely on algorithms, potentially overlooking certain subjective factors that human appraisers or wholesalers consider in property valuation.

2. Reliance on Data Accuracy: AVMs heavily depend on the accuracy and reliability of the data they utilize. Inaccurate or incomplete data can lead to incorrect valuation estimates.

3. Limited Scope: AVMs may struggle to accurately value unique or specialized properties that lack sufficient data or have complex characteristics.

4. Lack of Contextual Understanding: AVMs may not consider the specific local market dynamics or nuances that can influence property values, such as neighborhood changes or future development plans.

Technological tools, including AVMs, have transformed property valuation in real estate wholesaling. While AVMs offer efficiency, speed, and cost-effectiveness, they have limitations such as the lack of human judgment, reliance on accurate data, and limited scope for unique properties. Wholesalers should consider using AVMs as a helpful tool in combination with expert knowledge and judgment to make informed decisions. It is crucial to understand the strengths and weaknesses of AVMs and use them as part of a comprehensive approach to property valuation in wholesaling.

Understanding the Role of Professional Appraisals in Real Estate Valuation and Working with Appraisers

Professional appraisals play a crucial role in the real estate valuation process, providing an unbiased and expert opinion on property value. In this chapter, we will delve into the significance of professional appraisals and discuss how to effectively work with appraisers and understand their appraisal reports.

Role of Professional Appraisals in the Valuation Process:
Professional appraisals serve several key purposes in the real estate valuation process:

1. Objective Property Valuation: Appraisals provide an unbiased and independent assessment of a property's value based on various factors, such as location, condition, amenities, market trends, and comparable sales data. They help establish a fair and accurate market value.

2. Lender Requirement: Appraisals are often required by lenders before approving a mortgage loan. Lenders want to ensure that the property's value aligns with the loan amount.

3. Risk Mitigation: Appraisals help mitigate risks for buyers, sellers, lenders, and investors by providing an objective evaluation of the property. They assist in identifying potential issues, such as overvalued or undervalued properties, and help in making informed decisions.

How to Work with Appraisers and Understand Appraisal Reports:

1. Engage in Effective Communication: Maintain open and transparent communication with the appraiser. Provide complete and accurate information about the property, including any recent upgrades, renovations, or unique features.

2. Accompany the Appraiser: Offer to accompany the appraiser during the property inspection. This allows you to point out any relevant information, features, or improvements that may impact the valuation.

3. Provide Comparable Sales Data: If you have access to recent comparable sales in the area, provide them to the appraiser. This information can support the appraiser's analysis and provide additional insights into the property's value.

4. Review and Understand the Appraisal Report:

- Property Description: The appraisal report includes a detailed description of the property, including its size, condition, layout, and notable features.
- Comparable Sales Analysis: The report should include a comparative analysis of recent sales of similar properties in the area, demonstrating how they influenced the appraised value.
- Adjustments: Appraisers may make adjustments to the comparable sales data to account for differences in size, condition, or other relevant factors. Review these adjustments to understand their impact on the final value.
- Valuation Conclusion: The appraisal report will include the final estimated value of the property based on the appraiser's analysis.

5. Seek Clarification if Needed: If you have any questions or concerns regarding the appraisal report, don't hesitate to seek clarification from the appraiser. It's essential to fully understand the factors considered and the reasoning behind the appraised value.

Professional appraisals are integral to the real estate valuation process, providing unbiased and expert opinions on property value. By effectively working with appraisers and understanding their appraisal reports, you can gain valuable insights into the property's value and make informed decisions. Maintaining open communication, providing relevant information, and reviewing the appraisal report diligently are key steps in ensuring a smooth appraisal process.

Understanding Valuation Adjustments and Their Application in Real Estate

Valuation adjustments are essential in the real estate valuation process to account for various factors that can influence a property's value. In this chapter, we will explore the factors that may require adjustments in valuations, such as market conditions, property condition, and location. We will also discuss how to quantify and apply these adjustments effectively.

Factors that Require Adjustments in Valuations:

1. Market Conditions: Changes in the real estate market can significantly impact property values. Factors such as supply and demand, economic conditions, interest rates, and local market trends may necessitate adjustments. For example, during a seller's market where demand exceeds supply, valuations may require upward adjustments, whereas in a buyer's market, adjustments may be downwards.

2. Property Condition: The condition of a property can greatly influence its value. Adjustments are necessary to account for differences in the overall condition, age, maintenance, and upgrades of the property. A well-maintained and updated property may require upward adjustments, while a property in need of repairs or renovations may require downward adjustments.

3. Location: The location of a property is a significant determinant of its value. Adjustments are made based on factors such as proximity to amenities (schools, parks, shopping centers), access to transportation, desirability of the neighborhood, and overall location quality. Desirable locations may require upward adjustments, while less desirable or remote locations may require downward adjustments.

How to Quantify and Apply Adjustments:

1. Comparative Market Analysis (CMA): Conduct a thorough comparative market analysis to identify comparable properties that have recently sold in the area. This analysis helps establish a baseline value and provides a framework for applying adjustments.

2. Selection of Comparable Properties: Choose comparable properties that are similar to the subject property in terms of size, location, amenities, and condition. The closer the resemblance, the more accurate the adjustments are likely to be.

3. Adjustments Analysis: Compare the subject property to the chosen comps and identify key differences that require adjustments. For example, if the subject property has an additional bedroom compared to the comps, an adjustment may be required to account for the difference in value.

4. Quantifying Adjustments: The adjustment amount is determined by analyzing market data, consulting with industry professionals, and considering the local market conditions. The adjustments can be expressed as a percentage or a dollar amount, depending on the specific factor being adjusted.

5. Applying Adjustments: Apply the quantified adjustments to the comparable properties, either by adding or subtracting from their sale

prices. This provides a more accurate reflection of the subject property's value.

6. Reconciliation: After applying adjustments to each comparable property, analyze the adjusted sale prices to determine a final value range for the subject property. Consider the overall trends in the market and weigh the adjustments accordingly to arrive at a reconciled estimate of value.

Valuation adjustments are essential to account for factors such as market conditions, property condition, and location that can influence a property's value. Through proper analysis, quantification, and application of adjustments, real estate professionals can provide more accurate and reliable valuations. Understanding the specific factors that require adjustments and considering the nuances of the local market conditions are key to conducting a comprehensive and effective valuation process.

Avoiding Common Valuation Mistakes: Being Conservative and Realistic

Property valuation requires careful analysis and consideration to provide accurate and reliable assessments. However, there are common pitfalls that can lead to inaccurate valuations. In this chapter, we will explore these pitfalls and discuss strategies to avoid them. We will also emphasize the importance of adopting a conservative and realistic approach to valuation assessments.

Common Pitfalls in Property Valuation and How to Avoid Them:

1. Over Reliance on Comparable Sales: Relying solely on comparable sales without considering other factors can lead to flawed valuations. Avoid this by conducting a comprehensive analysis that takes into

account the property's unique characteristics, market conditions, location, and physical condition.

2. Ignoring Market Trends: Failing to consider current market trends can result in inaccurate valuations. Stay updated on market conditions, including supply and demand dynamics, interest rates, economic factors, and local developments. Incorporate this information into your valuation assessments.

3. Neglecting Property-Specific Factors: Each property has distinctive features that can impact its value. Pay attention to factors such as size, layout, condition, amenities, age, and upgrades. Ignoring these details can lead to disparities between the subject property and comparable sales.

4. Lack of Local Market Knowledge: Valuation assessments should be grounded in an understanding of the local market. Familiarize yourself with the neighborhood dynamics, community amenities, school districts, transportation accessibility, and other relevant factors. This knowledge will enhance the accuracy of your valuations.

5. Failing to Account for Future Developments: Overlooking potential future developments in the area can result in valuation errors. Consider upcoming infrastructure projects, zoning changes, and urban planning initiatives that may influence the property's value in the future.

Importance of Being Conservative and Realistic in Valuation Assessments:

1. Risk Mitigation: Adopting a conservative approach helps mitigate risk by avoiding inflated valuations. Understating the property's value offers a buffer against market fluctuations and unforeseen circumstances.

2. Realistic Expectations: Realistic valuations set realistic expectations for buyers, sellers, lenders, and investors. Unrealistically high valuations can create false perceptions and lead to disappointment or challenges during transactions.

3. Long-Term Investments: Valuing properties conservatively is especially crucial for long-term investments. Overvaluing a property may lead to financial strain, especially if rental income or property appreciation does not match the inflated valuation.

4. Credibility and Trust: As a valuer, maintaining credibility and trust is vital. Providing realistic and transparent valuations builds trust with clients and stakeholders, establishing a reputation for reliability and professionalism.

Avoiding common valuation mistakes is essential to provide accurate and reliable assessments. By considering factors beyond comparable sales, staying informed about market trends, understanding local market dynamics, and adopting a conservative and realistic approach, you can enhance the accuracy of your valuations. Remember, being conservative helps mitigate risks, establishes realistic expectations, and fosters credibility in the valuation profession.

Advanced Valuation Techniques:

Discounted Cash Flow Analysis and Scenario Analysis

In addition to traditional valuation methods, advanced techniques provide a deeper understanding of a property's value. In this chapter, we will introduce two such methods: discounted cash flow (DCF) analysis and scenario analysis. These techniques offer valuable insights by incorporating future cash flows and considering various scenarios that can impact a property's value.

Discounted Cash Flow (DCF) Analysis:

Discounted cash flow analysis is a method used to estimate the value of an investment based on its projected future cash flows. It takes into account the time value of money, considering that the value of money decreases over time due to inflation and other factors. Here's how DCF analysis works:

1. Cash Flow Projections: Forecast the expected future cash inflows and outflows associated with the property over a specific period. This may include rental income, operating expenses, taxes, and capital expenditures.

2. Discount Rate: Determine an appropriate discount rate, which reflects the risk and return expectations of the investment. The discount rate adjusts the future cash flows to their present value, considering the time value of money.

3. Net Present Value (NPV): Calculate the net present value by subtracting the present value of cash outflows from the present value of cash inflows. A positive NPV indicates that the investment is potentially value-generating.

4. Sensitivity Analysis: Evaluate the sensitivity of the valuation to changes in key assumptions (e.g., rental growth rate, discount rate, occupancy rate). This analysis helps understand the impact of varying factors on the property's value.

Scenario Analysis:

Scenario analysis involves examining the potential impact of different scenarios on a property's value. It helps develop a better understanding of the property's sensitivity to various market conditions, risks, and opportunities. Here's how scenario analysis is applied:

1. Identify Scenarios: Determine relevant scenarios that may impact the property's value and cash flows. For example, scenarios might include optimistic, base, and pessimistic scenarios based on market conditions or specific events.

2. Quantify Assumptions: Assign specific assumptions to each scenario, such as rental growth rates, vacancy rates, interest rates, or economic indicators. These assumptions should be realistic and reflect the conditions under each scenario.

3. Valuation Analysis: Apply the valuation methodology (such as DCF analysis) to each scenario to determine the property's value under different circumstances. Compare the results to assess the potential impact of each scenario.

4. Risk Assessment and Decision Making: Analyze the range of potential values and associated risks to make informed decisions. Understanding the property's performance across different scenarios helps assess risk exposure and devise appropriate risk management strategies.

Advanced valuation techniques, such as discounted cash flow analysis and scenario analysis, provide a more comprehensive understanding of a property's value. By incorporating future cash flows, adjusting for the time value of money, and considering various scenarios, these techniques allow for a more nuanced valuation approach. Leveraging these advanced techniques enhances decision-making, risk assessment, and strategic planning within the real estate industry.

Title: Using Valuation in Negotiations: Leveraging Accuracy for Effective Outcomes

Introduction:
Accurate valuations play a crucial role in negotiation settings, enabling parties to make informed decisions and achieve mutually beneficial outcomes. In this chapter, we will explore how to leverage accurate valuations during negotiations and provide case studies that showcase the effectiveness of using solid valuation data.

Leveraging Accurate Valuations in Negotiation Settings:

1. Establishing Credibility: A well-prepared and accurate valuation report enhances your credibility during negotiations. It showcases your expertise and provides a solid foundation for your arguments, increasing the likelihood of gaining trust and respect from all parties involved.

2. Objective Pricing: Accurate valuations provide an objective basis for pricing discussions. By relying on credible valuation data, negotiations can move beyond subjective opinions and focus on the actual value of the property or asset. This facilitates productive and data-driven negotiations.

3. Understanding Negotiation Leverage: Accurate valuations empower you to understand your negotiation leverage. You can assess the relative strengths and weaknesses of each party's position based on the valuation data. This knowledge allows you to approach negotiations strategically and make informed decisions.

4. Identifying Win-Win Opportunities: By having a clear understanding of a property's value, negotiations can explore win-win opportunities. Accurate valuations enable parties to identify creative solutions that

maximize value for all involved, leading to mutually beneficial outcomes.

Case Studies Demonstrating Effective Negotiation Using Solid Valuation Data:

1. Residential Property Sale: A buyer and seller were negotiating the sale price of a residential property. The buyer used a comprehensive valuation report, considering the property's condition, comparable sales, and market trends. Armed with accurate data, the buyer was able to convince the seller of a fair market value, resulting in a successful negotiation and a win-win outcome.

2. Commercial Lease Renewal: A tenant and landlord were negotiating the renewal terms of a commercial lease. The tenant presented a valuation analysis showcasing the property's market rental rates, occupancy rates, and other financial metrics. With solid valuation data, the tenant negotiated a favorable lease renewal with reduced rental costs, aligned with the property's true value.

3. Business Acquisition: During the negotiation of a business acquisition, both parties relied on comprehensive valuations of the business, including its assets, revenue projections, and market competition. This allowed for fact-based discussions, agreement on a fair purchase price, and the successful completion of the acquisition.

Leveraging accurate valuations in negotiation settings can significantly impact outcomes. By establishing credibility, enabling objective pricing discussions, understanding negotiation leverage, and identifying win-win opportunities, parties can negotiate with confidence and transparency. The case studies presented exemplify the value of using solid valuation data, leading to successful negotiations and mutually beneficial agreements. Incorporating accurate valuations into negotiation strategies enhances decision-making, fosters trust, and contributes to positive outcomes in various real estate and business transactions.

Conclusion: The Importance of Mastering Property Valuation

Valuation is a critical component of the real estate industry, and it plays a crucial role in determining property values, making informed investment decisions, and negotiating successful transactions. In this chapter's conclusion, we will recap the importance of mastering property valuation, and encourage continuous refinement of valuation skills for business success.

Importance of Mastering Property Valuation:

1. Accurate Property Valuation: The ability to accurately assess the value of properties is fundamental in the real estate industry. Conducting comprehensive valuation analyses enables informed decision-making, investment strategies, and effective negotiations.

2. Investment Decisions: Relying on accurate valuation data allows for informed investment decisions, mitigating risks, and maximizing return on investment. Understanding risk tolerance and the economic environment helps determine the property's long-term earning potential and aligns investment goals with market realities.

3. Negotiations: Valuation reports provide a reliable basis for negotiations, enabling parties to leverage factual data, establish credibility, and identify optimal solutions. Mastery of property valuation techniques furnishes real estate professionals with the aptitude necessary to negotiate successfully.

Continuous Refinement of Valuation Skills:

The real estate industry is dynamic, and changes to local markets and global economies continuously influence asset values. Continuous investment in improving valuation skills is crucial to remain competitive. Some ways to improve valuation skills include:

1. Staying Up-to-Date with Market Trends: Keeping an eye on trends, market analyses, and industry developments is vital. Professional associations, local market reports, and industry publications are excellent resources to stay informed.

2. Refining Technical Skills: Engaging in additional valuation training programs, attending industry conferences, and working with experienced professionals provide opportunities to develop technical expertise.

3. Leveraging Technology: Utilizing advanced tools such as data analysis platforms, artificial intelligence, and machine learning can provide deeper insights and improve overall valuation accuracy.

4. Collaborating with Peers: Networking, exchanging knowledge and experiences among industry peers is valuable for professional development.

Encouragement to Continuously Refine Valuation Skills for Business Success:

In conclusion, mastering property valuation techniques is crucial for achieving success in the real estate industry. Continuous investment in refining valuation skills and embracing emerging valuation technologies ensures a competitive edge. As the industry landscape shifts, keen valuation skills and expertise are essential to maximize opportunities and catalyze business success.

Conclusion: Seizing Success in Real Estate Wholesaling

Recap of Key Lessons:

Real estate investing can be a rewarding venture, but it requires a solid understanding of key strategies and concepts to achieve long-term success and mitigate risks. Throughout this book, we have explored essential strategies that serve as the building blocks for a prosperous career in real estate wholesaling. In this recap, we will summarize the key lessons covered and highlight the importance of understanding legal frameworks, market dynamics, and financial management in the pursuit of real estate success.

I. Understanding Legal Frameworks:
A. Familiarize Yourself with Real Estate Laws:
- Recap the importance of comprehending federal, state, and local laws governing real estate transactions.
- Emphasize the significance of conducting thorough due diligence to ensure compliance with legal requirements.

B. Develop a Solid Contractual Foundation:
- Highlight the essential components of a real estate contract, such as parties involved, purchase price, and contingency clauses.
- Explain the significance of contract negotiation and effective communication to protect your interests and avoid potential disputes.

II. Mastering Market Dynamics:

A. Conducting Market Research:
- Summarize the process of researching and analyzing local real estate markets, including factors like supply and demand, demographics, and economic indicators.
- Discuss the importance of staying informed about market trends to identify lucrative opportunities and make informed investment decisions.

B. Building Relationships with Key Stakeholders:
- Emphasize the importance of networking and establishing connections with real estate agents, wholesalers, investors, and other professionals in the industry.
- Highlight the benefits of collaboration and knowledge-sharing to stay ahead of market developments and maximize investment potential.

III. Financial Management:
A. Budgeting and Cash Flow Management:
- Summarize the significance of budgeting and creating a comprehensive financial plan to analyze income and expenses accurately.
- Discuss strategies to manage cash flow effectively, including setting aside reserves for unexpected expenses and maximizing profitability.

B. Financing Options and Strategies:
- Provide an overview of financing options such as traditional loans, private lenders, and partnerships.
- Explore creative financing strategies like wholesaling, flipping, and lease options to optimize returns and minimize financial risks.

C. Risk Management and Exit Strategies:
- Explain the importance of assessing and managing risks associated with real estate investments, such as market fluctuations and property-specific challenges.

- Discuss various exit strategies, including selling, renting, or refinancing properties, to adapt to changing market conditions and achieve long-term financial goals.

Real estate wholesaling presents opportunities for financial success, but it requires a comprehensive understanding of legal frameworks, market dynamics, and effective financial management. In this recap, we explored the key lessons covered in this book, emphasizing the importance of legality, market research, networking, budgeting, financing, and risk management. By applying these strategies, aspiring real estate investors can seize success and build a solid foundation for a prosperous future in the dynamic world of real estate wholesaling.

The Mindset of a Successful Wholesaler:

Wholesaling is a dynamic and challenging business that requires a particular mindset to achieve success. In this chapter, we will discuss the essential qualities that define successful wholesalers, with a focus on persistence, resilience, and adaptability. We will also explore the value of embracing a mindset of continuous learning and improvement to stay ahead of the curve and overcome obstacles in the fast-paced world of real estate wholesaling.

I. Persistence:
A. Embrace the Importance of Persistence:
- Discuss how persistence in reaching out to potential sellers and negotiating deals is essential for wholesaling success.
- Highlight the significance of developing a robust work ethic to achieve long-term goals and overcome challenges.

B. Strategies for Maintaining Persistence:

- Offer tips for staying motivated when facing rejection, such as setting realistic goals and taking strategic breaks to refresh and refocus.
- Emphasize the importance of cultivating a positive mindset to stay optimistic and confident in the face of obstacles.

II. Resilience:
A. The Role of Resilience in Wholesaling:
- Define resilience as the ability to bounce back from adversity and overcome challenges.
- Explain how resilience is crucial for handling unexpected setbacks and adapting to changing market conditions.

B. Strategies for Building Resilience:
- Offer tips for fostering resilience, such as developing a support network, practicing self-care, and maintaining a growth mindset.
- Encourage wholesalers to see challenges as opportunities for growth and learning, rather than setbacks.

III. Adaptability:
A. The Importance of Adaptability:
- Define adaptability as the ability to adjust to changing circumstances and develop creative solutions to problems.
- Discuss how adaptability is essential for navigating the fast-changing real estate market and seizing new opportunities.

B. Strategies for Building Adaptability:
- Offer tips for fostering adaptability, such as staying informed about market trends and developments, seeking innovative solutions to problems, and embracing change.
- Encourage wholesalers to stay curious and open to new ideas, and to seek out opportunities to learn and grow in their field.

IV. A Mindset of Continuous Learning and Improvement:
A. The Value of Lifelong Learning:

- Explain the importance of continuous learning and personal growth for wholesaling success.
- Discuss how staying informed about market trends, developing new skills, and seeking out mentorship can help wholesalers stay ahead of the curve and seize opportunities for growth.

B. Strategies for Lifelong Learning:
- Offer tips for building a mindset of continuous learning, such as investing in education and training, seeking mentorship, and attending industry events and conferences.
- Encourage wholesalers to develop a passion for their work, stay enthusiastic about their field, and never stop seeking opportunities to improve and grow.

A successful wholesaler requires a particular mindset that encompasses persistence, resilience, adaptability, and a lifelong commitment to learning and personal growth. In this chapter, we have explored the essential qualities that define successful wholesalers, emphasizing the importance of staying motivated, bouncing back from adversity, adapting to change, and never stopping the pursuit of improvement and growth. By embracing these qualities, aspiring wholesalers can develop the mindset and skills needed to achieve long-term success and prosper in the dynamic world of real estate wholesaling.

Overcoming Common Challenges:
The journey of a real estate wholesaler is not without its fair share of challenges. In this chapter, we will revisit common obstacles that wholesalers face and explore strategies to overcome them. We will also provide motivational insights to inspire confidence, even in tough market conditions. By developing resilience and implementing effective problem-solving techniques, wholesalers can navigate these challenges with confidence and emerge stronger in their pursuit of success.

I. Dealing with Seller Resistance:

A. Understanding Seller Concerns:
- Revisit common seller concerns and objections, such as price, property condition, and trust issues.
- Discuss the importance of empathizing with sellers' perspectives and addressing their concerns effectively.

B. Strategies for Overcoming Seller Resistance:
- Offer negotiation techniques such as active listening, building rapport, and presenting win-win solutions.
- Emphasize the significance of effective communication and transparency in building trust with sellers.

II. Managing Cash Flow:
A. Cash Flow Challenges in Wholesaling:
- Revisit the common issue of managing cash flow, particularly when dealing with marketing expenses and contract commitments.
- Discuss the importance of budgeting and strategizing to ensure a consistent cash flow throughout the wholesaling process.

B. Strategies for Managing Cash Flow:
- Offer tips for budgeting and forecasting, such as tracking expenses, maximizing marketing ROI, and establishing financial reserves.
- Discuss creative financing options and partnerships to mitigate cash flow constraints.

III. Handling Market Volatility:
A. Embracing Changing Market Conditions:
- Revisit the challenges posed by market volatility, including fluctuating property prices and shifts in demand.
- Highlight the importance of staying informed and adaptable to navigate market changes effectively.

B. Strategies for Navigating Market Volatility:
- Encourage wholesalers to conduct thorough market research and analysis to identify emerging trends and opportunities.

- Explore diversification strategies and the importance of being open to different types of properties and locations.

IV. Cultivating Confidence in Tough Market Conditions:
A. Fostering a Positive Mindset:
- Discuss the power of positive thinking and self-belief in overcoming challenges.
- Encourage wholesalers to focus on their strengths, celebrate small victories, and stay resilient in the face of adversity.

B. Motivational Insights:
- Share inspiring stories and testimonials of successful wholesalers who overcame challenges to achieve remarkable success.
- Provide motivational quotes and insights to uplift wholesalers' spirits and inspire them to persevere through tough times.

Overcoming challenges is an inherent part of the real estate wholesaling journey. By revisiting common obstacles and implementing effective strategies, wholesalers can navigate seller resistance, manage cash flow, and adapt to changing market conditions. Moreover, by cultivating a positive mindset and drawing inspiration from motivational insights, wholesalers can develop the confidence needed to overcome any obstacles encountered along the way. With determination, resilience, and a relentless pursuit of success, wholesalers can thrive in even the toughest market conditions and achieve their goals in the dynamic world of real estate wholesaling.

Leveraging Networks and Relationships:

In the world of real estate wholesaling, building and nurturing strong professional relationships is crucial for business growth and success. In this chapter, we will explore the significance of leveraging networks and relationships and provide valuable tips for nurturing a robust network that can propel your business forward. By understanding the importance of genuine connections and implementing effective relationship-building strategies, wholesalers can tap into valuable resources, opportunities, and support to drive their business growth.

I. The Power of Relationships in Wholesaling:
A. Establishing Trust and Credibility:
- Emphasize the role of trust and credibility in building strong professional relationships.
- Discuss how establishing these qualities can lead to more opportunities and greater cooperation with partners, sellers, and buyers.

B. Accessing Valuable Resources:
- Highlight how a strong network can provide access to industry knowledge, market insights, and valuable contacts.
- Discuss the benefits of collaborating with like-minded professionals to share resources, strategies, and expertise.

II. Tips for Nurturing a Robust Network:
A. Attend Industry Events and Networking Functions:
- Encourage wholesalers to actively participate in real estate conferences, seminars, and networking events.
- Provide tips for engaging in meaningful conversations, exchanging contact information, and following up with potential connections.

B. Cultivate Genuine Relationships:
- Promote the idea of building authentic, long-term relationships based on trust, reciprocity, and mutual benefit.
- Highlight the importance of actively listening, demonstrating genuine interest, and offering support to others in the industry.

C. Utilize Online Platforms:

- Discuss the benefits of leveraging social media platforms, professional networking websites, and online communities.
- Provide tips for creating a strong online presence, engaging with industry professionals, and showcasing expertise.

D. Seek Mentorship and Guidance:
- Encourage wholesalers to seek mentorship from experienced professionals in the field.
- Discuss the value of learning from mentors' experiences, gaining insights, and accessing valuable guidance.

III. Maintaining and Strengthening Relationships:
A. Communication and Follow-Up:
- Stress the importance of regular communication and follow-up with contacts in your network.
- Provide tips for staying in touch, sending relevant updates, and expressing gratitude for the relationship.

B. Offer Support and Value:
- Discuss the benefits of being a valuable resource to your network by sharing knowledge, insights, and industry-related information.
- Encourage wholesalers to actively support and promote their connections' businesses to foster mutually beneficial relationships.

C. Attend Local Real Estate Associations and Meetups:
- Highlight the value of engaging with local real estate associations and attending meetups.
- Discuss the opportunities for networking, collaborating, and staying updated on local market trends.

Building and maintaining strong professional relationships is a key ingredient for success in the world of real estate wholesaling. By emphasizing trust, credibility, and access to resources, wholesalers can leverage their networks to propel their business growth. By attending industry events, cultivating genuine relationships, utilizing online platforms, seeking mentorship, and maintaining regular communication, wholesalers can nurture a robust network that will open doors to new opportunities, provide valuable support, and contribute to long-term success. With a focus on building meaningful connections, wholesalers can create a thriving network that becomes a powerful asset for their business endeavors.

Innovating and Scaling Your Business:

Scaling a real estate wholesaling business from a startup to a 7-figure enterprise requires a combination of strategic innovation and effective execution. In this chapter, we will explore key strategies for scaling your business, focusing on innovation in marketing, process automation, and diversifying investment strategies. By embracing innovation, implementing scalable processes, and exploring new avenues for growth, wholesalers can position themselves for exponential success in their journey towards building a thriving enterprise.

I. Scaling Strategies for Wholesalers:
A. Setting Clear Goals and Vision:
- Emphasize the importance of establishing clear business goals and a long-term vision for growth.
- Discuss the role of goal-setting in providing direction and focus during the scaling process.

B. Streamlining Processes and Automation:
- Discuss the benefits of streamlining operational processes and embracing automation tools.
- Explore strategies for automating lead generation, deal analysis, marketing campaigns, and administrative tasks.

C. Building a High-Performing Team:

- Highlight the significance of assembling a skilled and motivated team to support business growth.
- Discuss effective hiring practices, team development strategies, and fostering a culture of innovation and collaboration.

II. Innovation in Marketing:
A. Utilizing Digital Marketing Channels:
- Discuss the power of digital marketing in reaching a wider audience and generating quality leads.
- Highlight effective strategies for leveraging social media, search engine optimization (SEO), content marketing, and paid advertising.

B. Embracing Creative Marketing Tactics:
- Encourage wholesalers to think outside the box and adopt innovative marketing tactics to stand out from the competition.
- Discuss the benefits of using video marketing, virtual tours, influencer outreach, and targeted direct mail campaigns.

C. Personal Branding and Thought Leadership:
- Emphasize the importance of building a strong personal brand to establish credibility and attract potential partners and investors.
- Discuss the value of sharing industry insights, success stories, and thought leadership through content creation and public speaking.

III. Process Automation and Efficiency:
A. Implementing Technology Solutions:
- Explore various technology tools and software that can streamline and automate different aspects of the wholesaling business.
- Discuss the benefits of using customer relationship management (CRM) systems, project management tools, and data analytics platforms.

B. Standardizing Processes:
- Discuss the importance of standardizing workflows and documenting processes to ensure consistency and scalability.

- Highlight the benefits of creating standard operating procedures (SOPs) and regularly reviewing and optimizing them for efficiency.

IV. Diversifying Investment Strategies:
A. Exploring New Markets and Niches:
- Encourage wholesalers to consider expanding into new geographical markets or exploring niche segments within the real estate industry.
- Discuss the benefits of diversifying investment strategies to minimize risk and maximize opportunities for growth.

B. Partnering and Collaborating:
- Discuss the advantages of forming strategic partnerships and collaborations with other real estate professionals.
- Highlight the benefits of pooling resources, sharing expertise, and tapping into new networks for enhanced growth potential.

C. Exploring Alternative Investment Vehicles:
- Encourage wholesalers to explore alternative investment options such as crowdfunding, joint ventures, or real estate syndication.
- Discuss the benefits of diversifying investment portfolios and leveraging the expertise and resources of other investors.

Scaling a real estate wholesaling business from an ambitious startup to a thriving 7-figure enterprise requires a combination of innovative thinking, streamlined processes, and diversified investment strategies. By setting clear goals, embracing technology and automation, and exploring new marketing avenues, wholesalers can position themselves for accelerated growth. Through strategic partnerships, collaborations, and thought leadership, wholesalers can tap into new markets and opportunities. With a focus on innovation, efficiency, and adaptability, wholesalers can build a scalable business that thrives in a dynamic real estate industry.

Title: Staying Ahead of Market Trends: The Importance of Ongoing Education and Analysis

Introduction:
In the rapidly evolving world of real estate wholesaling, staying ahead of market trends and regulatory changes is essential for success. In this chapter, we will explore the importance of ongoing education and market analysis, highlighting the resources and tools available to wholesalers to stay informed and capitalize on emerging opportunities. By staying up-to-date with the latest industry developments, wholesalers can position themselves to make informed decisions, adapt to changing market conditions, and achieve sustainable growth over the long term.

I. The Importance of Staying Informed:
A. Understanding Real Estate Market Trends:
- Emphasize the significance of staying informed about emerging real estate market trends, including changes in supply and demand, buyer preferences, and macroeconomic factors.
- Highlight the benefits of leveraging industry reports, surveys, and research publications to stay informed about market developments.

B. Keeping Up with Regulatory Changes:
- Discuss the significance of staying informed about regulatory changes and policy updates that can impact the real estate industry.
- Highlight the role of industry associations and professional networks in disseminating regulatory information to members.

II. Resources for Ongoing Education and Market Analysis:
A. Industry Associations and Networks:
- Explore the role and benefits of joining industry associations and professional networks in staying informed about the latest industry trends and developments.
- Highlight industry groups like the National Association of Realtors (NAR), Real Estate Investors Association (REIA), and Real Estate Wholesaling Association (REWA).

B. Educational Institutions and Training Programs:

- Discuss the benefits of formal and informal education, such as attending real estate courses, seminars, and workshops.
- Highlight online training platforms, certification programs, and continuing education credits.

C. Market Analysis Tools and Resources:
- Explore the tools available to wholesalers to conduct market analysis, including data analytics platforms, market research reports, and news outlets.
- Highlight resources such as Zillow, Redfin, Realtor.com, and local MLS services.

III. Strategies for Leveraging Market Trends:

A. Adapting to Emerging Demand:
- Discuss the importance of anticipating and adapting to emerging buyer preferences and market demands.
- Highlight the benefits of leveraging data analytics and market research to identify lucrative opportunities in the real estate market.

B. Innovating and Diversifying:
- Highlight the value of adopting innovative business models and diversifying investment strategies to stay ahead of the competition.
- Encourage wholesalers to leverage emerging technologies, explore new markets, and diversify their real estate investment portfolio.

C. Building a Strong Professional Network:
- Emphasize the role of building strong professional relationships in staying informed about the latest industry trends and opportunities.
- Explore strategies for networking, collaborating, and sharing resources with other real estate professionals.

Staying ahead of real estate market trends and regulatory changes is a crucial aspect of success in real estate wholesaling. By staying informed through ongoing education and market analysis, wholesalers can make informed decisions, adapt to changing market conditions, and capitalize on emerging opportunities. Through membership in industry associations, attending training programs, and leveraging market analysis resources, wholesalers can stay on the cutting edge of knowledge and insight. With a focus on innovation, adaptability, and building strong professional relationships, wholesalers can position themselves for sustained success in the dynamic real estate industry.

Commitment to Ethical Practices

In the competitive landscape of real estate wholesaling, a strong commitment to ethical practices is not only essential for building a sustainable business but also for differentiating yourself from competitors. In this chapter, we will reiterate the importance of integrity and ethics, highlighting how ethical practices can elevate your business and establish a reputation for trustworthiness and professionalism. By prioritizing ethical decision-making, wholesalers can foster long-term relationships, attract loyal customers, and create a competitive advantage in the market.

I. The Importance of Integrity and Ethics:
A. Upholding Professionalism and Trust:
- Emphasize the significance of conducting business with integrity, honesty, and transparency.
- Discuss how ethical practices contribute to building trust with clients, partners, and the broader community.

B. Long-term Sustainability:
- Highlight the benefits of prioritizing ethical practices in establishing a long-term sustainable business.
- Discuss how a reputation for integrity can attract repeat customers and referrals, leading to a solid foundation for growth.

II. Differentiating Your Business:
A. Building a Strong Reputation:

- Discuss how ethical practices can differentiate your business by creating a strong reputation for trustworthiness and reliability.
- Emphasize the importance of positive word-of-mouth referrals and online reviews in attracting new customers.

B. Attracting Loyal Customers:
- Highlight how ethical practices can foster customer loyalty and improve customer satisfaction.
- Discuss the value of exceptional customer service, fair dealings, and transparent communication in building long-term relationships.

C. Standing Out in a Competitive Market:
- Explore how ethical practices can help your business stand out in a crowded marketplace.
- Highlight the benefits of a strong ethical foundation in attracting clients who value integrity and are willing to pay a premium for ethical business practices.

III. Implementing Ethical Practices:
A. Code of Conduct and Ethical Guidelines:
- Discuss the importance of developing a comprehensive code of conduct and ethical guidelines that define acceptable business practices.
- Encourage wholesalers to communicate and educate their team members about these guidelines.

B. Transparent Communication:
- Highlight the significance of transparent and honest communication with all stakeholders: clients, partners, employees, and regulatory authorities.
- Discuss the benefits of setting realistic expectations, providing accurate information, and addressing concerns promptly.

C. Compliance with Laws and Regulations:

- Emphasize the importance of complying with applicable laws, regulations, and industry standards.
- Discuss the value of staying informed about legal and regulatory changes that can impact the real estate industry.

A strong commitment to ethical practices is not only a moral imperative but also a strategic advantage in real estate wholesaling. By prioritizing integrity and ethics, wholesalers can differentiate their business, build a strong reputation, and attract loyal customers. Ethical practices contribute to long-term sustainability and foster trust with clients and partners, setting the stage for growth and success. By implementing ethical guidelines, fostering transparent communication, and staying compliant with laws and regulations, wholesalers can establish themselves as leaders in the industry who prioritize the highest standards of professionalism and integrity.

Future Outlook in Real Estate Wholesaling:

The real estate wholesaling industry is poised for exciting opportunities and advancements in the future. In this chapter, we will offer insights into the future outlook of the real estate market and the potential for wholesalers. We will discuss the importance of embracing changes and technological advancements to stay ahead of the curve. By adapting and leveraging emerging trends, wholesalers can position themselves for success in the evolving landscape of real estate wholesaling.

I. Evolving Real Estate Market:
A. Demographic Shifts and Changing Buyer Preferences:
- Discuss how demographic shifts, such as the rise of millennial homebuyers and changing buyer preferences, are shaping the real estate market.
- Emphasize the need for wholesalers to adapt their strategies to cater to the evolving needs and preferences of the market.

B. Market Accessibility and Globalization:
- Highlight the increasing accessibility of real estate markets through technological advancements and globalization.
- Discuss the potential for wholesalers to tap into international markets and capitalize on emerging opportunities.

II. Technological Advancements:

A. Automation and AI:
- Explore the impact of automation and artificial intelligence on real estate wholesaling.
- Discuss the potential for streamlining processes, analyzing market data, and improving operational efficiency through AI-powered tools and platforms.

B. Virtual Reality (VR) and Augmented Reality (AR):
- Discuss the role of VR and AR in transforming the way properties are showcased to potential buyers.
- Highlight the potential for wholesalers to leverage these technologies for virtual property tours, staging, and remote collaboration.

C. Blockchain and Smart Contracts:
- Explore the potential applications of blockchain technology and smart contracts in real estate transactions and property ownership.
- Discuss how wholesalers can benefit from increased security, transparency, and efficiency in their business operations.

III. Embracing Opportunities and Adapting to Change:

A. Continuous Learning and Skill Development:
- Encourage wholesalers to embrace a mindset of continuous learning and skill development to stay abreast of industry advancements.
- Discuss the importance of attending conferences, workshops, and online courses to expand knowledge and adapt to changing trends.

B. Leveraging Data Analytics and Market Research:

- Highlight the importance of leveraging data analytics and market research to make informed decisions and identify profitable opportunities.
- Discuss the potential of big data analytics and predictive modeling in predicting market trends and optimizing investment strategies.

C. Collaboration and Partnerships:
- Emphasize the value of collaboration and partnerships in the future of real estate wholesaling.
- Discuss the potential for working with technology providers, real estate professionals, and industry experts to leverage collective knowledge and resources.

The future of real estate wholesaling promises exciting opportunities for those who are willing to adapt, embrace changes, and leverage technological advancements. By understanding the evolving real estate market, embracing emerging technologies, and continuously learning and evolving, wholesalers can position themselves for success. It is essential to stay informed about demographic shifts, changing buyer preferences, and global market trends. By leveraging automation, AI, VR, AR, blockchain, and smart contracts, wholesalers can streamline processes, enhance customer experiences, and improve operational efficiency. Embracing the future outlook in real estate wholesaling is not only essential for growth but also for staying ahead in a dynamic and competitive industry.

Building a successful real estate wholesaling business is a fulfilling and rewarding journey. In this final section, we would like to provide words of encouragement to inspire and motivate you to take action. We want to remind you of the incredible potential within the real estate industry and the opportunities that lie ahead. Remember, with dedication, perseverance, and a positive mindset, you can create a thriving and prosperous business.

I. Embrace the Journey:
A. Embrace Challenges as Learning Opportunities:
- Recognize that challenges are stepping stones towards growth and success.
- Embrace setbacks with resilience and use them as opportunities to learn, adapt and improve your strategies.

B. Stay Passionate and Focused:
- Cultivate and maintain a deep passion for real estate wholesaling.
- Stay focused on your goals during tough times, reminding yourself why you started on this journey.

C. Surround Yourself with a Supportive Network:
- Seek out mentors, colleagues, and like-minded individuals who can offer guidance and support.
- Embrace collaboration and surround yourself with a supportive network that shares your entrepreneurial spirit.

II. Take Action:
A. Be Proactive and Persistent:
- Take consistent action towards your goals, even if progress may seem slow at times.
- Stay persistent, knowing that every step forward brings you closer to your vision of success.

B. Embrace New Opportunities:
- Be open to exploring new opportunities and adapting to the ever-evolving real estate industry.

- Embrace technological advancements and leverage them to your advantage.

C. Continual Learning and Growth:
- Commit to continuous learning and personal growth.
- Stay curious and seek knowledge in areas such as market trends, negotiation skills, and emerging strategies.

III. Celebrate Your Successes:
A. Recognize Milestones and Achievements:
- Celebrate and acknowledge your milestones and achievements along the way.
- Take pride in your successes, no matter how big or small they may seem.

B. Inspire and Pay It Forward:
- Share your experiences and knowledge with others to inspire and uplift them.
- Support fellow entrepreneurs and contribute to the growth of the real estate wholesaling community.

As you embark on this journey of building a successful real estate wholesaling business, remember that success is not just a destination but a continuous process of growth and improvement. Embrace challenges, stay passionate, and surround yourself with a supportive network. Take action, adapt to changes, and continually learn and grow. Celebrate your successes and inspire others along the way. The road to success may have ups and downs, but with determination and perseverance, you can create a thriving business and shape a prosperous future. Believe in yourself and let your entrepreneurial spirit soar. Best of luck on your rewarding journey of real estate wholesaling!

www.ingramcontent.com/pod-product-compliance
Lightning Source LLC
Chambersburg PA
CBHW052147220526
45471CB00004B/1570